CW01648301

Rail Table

by

Sue Cooke

Copyright © 2017 Sue Cooke

All rights reserved.

ISBN: 1979956987
ISBN-13: 978-1979956987

ONE

'I think this has been a big mistake.' It was a statement made to sound like a question, the way young people do, by raising their voice at the end of the sentence. 'The bloke's an idiot mum.' Definitely a statement. 'I just don't get it, you and him, I just don't get it.'

'Archie's a very nice man.'

'He's a fucking embarrassment.'

Alison watched as her daughter continued to display her outrage with noise and gesticulation, reminiscent of her father when he had a point to prove. Inherited bad behaviour was something Alison was working on with Lauren, with the added bonus that if Robert was exhibiting any bad behaviour at all these days, it certainly wasn't directed towards them.

The dynamic in the room shifted as Lauren's irritation with her mother, temporarily, transferred to the padlock on her suitcase. Alison suddenly became grateful for the poor workmanship of a cheap device that was bought simply because of its dazzling colour. She remained silent throughout her daughter's display, just as she used to do when her, now ex- husband, exhibited similar impatience. Intimidation can take many forms, Alison had discovered. With much practice over the years she had found it was better to quietly wait until things had calmed a little or Robert became embarrassed by the exaggerated animation of his argument.

Alison moved to gently close the balcony doors. Not just in the hope that she could protect Archie's feelings as he walked in the gardens below, but because the afternoon was hot and as the Caribbean sun streamed into the room the air conditioning fought back noisily. She would never want to hurt Archie, different to Robert in every way, because it was Archie who had saved her after the divorce.

Good, kind Archie. After a few moments the temperature began to drop and Alison dared to return to the conversation.

'Don't you think you're being a little unkind my dear?'

'Mum he's an arse.' Lauren was turning the contents of her suitcase onto the bed. 'God, I was sure I'd packed my phone charger. Mum did you bring yours?' Alison watched in silence. 'Mum this is really important you know.'

'I know but I'm sure it's in there somewhere.'

'Really helpful mum' snorted Lauren, 'really fucking helpful.'

'Look Lauren, could you just drop the expletives please, you know how much I hate it. Whether you like it or not we are going to be sharing this room and I don't know how I'm going to cope with a "fucking" here and an "arse" there.'

'Don't swear mum. You've never done it and to be honest I think it's too late for you to start and anyway it just doesn't sound right coming from you.' Lauren's hand shot down between an over-stuffed make-up bag and a pair of glitter flip-flops and pulled out her phone charger. Alison felt, for the moment at least, the crisis was over and moved out onto the balcony where she closed her eyes and let the sun warm her face.

Secretly she had always known that once the idea of a winter sun holiday had worn off, Lauren would, predictably, wriggle on the hook but by then it was booked and as Archie was paying there was no going back. "Archie's treat" he would say, and so he had selected the small island of Nevis in the hope that Lauren would be unable to avoid him for long.

Lauren's opinion of Archie hadn't really changed over the last three years since he had first appeared as her mother's employer. The antithesis of her father, Lauren had decided there was no place for him in their lives. Perhaps Alison should have tackled her daughter back then and asked for a little more respect but they were still getting used to their new roles since Robert had left. Neither knew quite how to behave. They were learning as they went along and sometimes they got it wrong. So when Archie became more than her employer Alison hesitated in telling her daughter, until one Sunday afternoon when Lauren arrived home unexpectedly and found them both in the bath. Alison was horrified and tried to catch her daughter before she ran from the house. However the bath excursion had been a bit of a tight squeeze and it took rather longer to extricate herself than she expected. Within minutes Lauren was on her way over to north London to spend the evening with her father, claiming to have been scarred for life by the experience.

Robert's approach with Lauren had been better than Alison had anticipated. He calmed her down, gave her a bed for the night and suggested it was a good thing that "mum was getting her life back together". Whilst it was novel to get her ex-husband's support she also thought that perhaps Robert's new, young wife hadn't much liked the idea of Lauren moving in. Alison had hated him for what he had done to their family but moreover she had hated him for doing it with someone less than half her age. There had been no easy way to get over her husband setting up home with a girl whose remedy for the morning after the night before was taking the stairs instead of the lift.

There was a knock at the bedroom door and a few moments later Lauren appeared on the balcony holding two tall glasses filled with rum punch, paper umbrellas and large chunks of pineapple.

'Compliments of the Management. If you can't finish yours leave it for me.' She smiled at her mother who wondered why it was children were always in denial when it came to whether their parents could have a good time, or finish their drinks, or stay up late into the night.

'It looks delicious, let's have them out here.' There was a slight breeze and it ruffled the bougainvillea on its way over the balcony, tossing the pink and purple flowers against the white walls of the building. Below them the gardens were strewn with avenues of palm trees in a very ordered design all the way down to the beach. Beyond the beach the Caribbean Sea sparkled endlessly into the distance, until it surrendered to a vivid blue sky. 'It's truly beautiful here.'

'They certainly do a good rum punch.' Lauren bit into the pineapple and threw the remains into her empty glass.

Alison was grateful for this middle ground where they could now meet. The divorce had fractured her family and she had watched as her daughter moved from bright, happy, child to disturbed teenager in the time it took her father to pack his bags and leave the house. Her daughter would never be the girl she once was but a lot of healing had taken place and Lauren was, at last, looking forward to her future. There was still the fallout from the divorce to contend with: Robert's new family and his obvious love for them, Lauren's manufactured bad-girl image that refused to go away, but generally Alison felt they were now okay and things could move on. Of course Lauren still missed seeing her father every day. He had always been her champion and the endless late night phone calls were a poor substitute.

Alison sometimes wondered if perhaps the age-gap between herself and Lauren had made things even more difficult. If she'd been a younger parent she might have supported her daughter better. Having a child at forty-two had made her an 'elderly primigravida' according to the hospital, a label Alison had come to detest. In fact anything with the word elderly attached to it was unwelcome. Although it had always seemed that Robert had no difficulty in identifying with the younger age group and their not too distant divorce had been an excellent example of that.

Looking across into the room Alison could see the bed littered with text books and papers, a reminder of her daughter's final exams, only months away. They were getting close now, the university had been chosen and Lauren had her heart set on a history degree. Alison would resolve the Archie/Lauren situation, she told herself, and not allow the holiday to turn into a war zone. Secretly though she did wonder whether Archie's idea of them all coming away together would really improve his relationship with her daughter. She looked at Lauren now, head back, jaw firmly set and she knew why she had her doubts.

People were moving around downstairs. It sounded like they were returning from the beach. There was a woman's voice and it carried easily on the breeze, an East coast American accent that was not without irritation.

'So you've done that then Jack?' she was asking. There was a low murmur, 'well okay, if you've done it, you've done it but you did ask, didn't you?' another low murmur. 'Okay, okay but you know you've gotta ask.' There was silence and then as if in desperation the American woman said 'alright, if you say it won't be a problem, it won't be a problem but you know I want a rail table tonight, Jack, you know that.'

'Mum, what's a rail table?' asked Lauren in a whisper.

'I've no idea darling but it's nice to hear someone else getting into trouble for a change.'

'You're not in trouble mum, not so long as you keep your boyfriend away from me.'

The sun had gone down but when Alison opened the door she felt the full force of the sultry Caribbean evening. She pulled at the skirt of her plain silk dress in desperation against the heat. It was hard to believe that twenty-four hours earlier she had stood shivering in the car park waiting to pick Lauren up from college. Waiting for Lauren was something Alison often found herself doing. Not even an eight hour flight and a four hour time difference was going to change that. Alison stood patiently in the doorway and behind her Lauren was dragging her feet and showing no signs of getting out of the room and going to dinner.

'I'm tired mum, what's the time at home?'

'It's seven here so it must be eleven o'clock at home.'

'Shit!'

'Oh Lauren what now?'

'Well I wanted to ring the twins, I promised dad.'

'Ring them in the morning, we really should go now.' Alison leaned against the door, holding it open as she waited and lifted her long black hair up off her neck in an attempt to cool down. In contrast to her mother Lauren exhibited complete control in one deft move by pulling her auburn hair back into a pony tail, wound it round her hand and fixed it on top of her head. Alison looked on in admiration and thought for the second time today how much the daughter resembled the father.

Outside it was dark and gentle noises floated on the air: the odd voice, the chirping of tiny bell frogs, the breeze forcing its way between the palm trees and the distant flip-flop of Lauren's footwear as she dragged along some way behind her mother.

Archie was already in the bar chatting to the other guests and Alison thought how like him that was, friendly, open and what a contrast to her daughter this evening. He looked freshly scrubbed but rather unkempt, as Archie often did, his shirt already half pulled out of his trousers and one of his laces undone as though he'd just run out of time.

'Here she is now' he was talking to an elderly woman next to him. He gave Alison a warm smile. 'You settled in alright? As you can see I've made friends already' he took her arm and guided her towards a chair next to him. 'This is Joan' he said gesturing towards the elderly woman who, although flanked by two sturdy walking sticks, appeared far too robust to need either of them, 'and her daughter Margaret'. Alison nodded at the beige woman sitting on the edge of her seat and decided Margaret looked like she might be more a sister than a daughter. 'This is Ali and,' he hesitated looking round for Lauren.

'She's just coming' said Alison apologetically.

'Here she is, better late than never, eh Lauren? This is Lauren.'

Lauren smiled weakly.

'Ah you have a grand-daughter' said the older woman smiling at Alison.

Archie laughed easily. 'No, Lauren is Ali's daughter.' He turned to Alison. 'They look more like sisters to me.' He was beaming now and Alison felt her face begin to flush. Musicians played jazz in the bar as they chatted and there was a buzz about the place that made Alison feel like she was at the beginning of something special.

The restaurant was quiet as they weaved their way between the tables to the very front of the room, a dark wood floor announcing their entrance. The candlelight bounced off the silver and glass carefully set on white damask tablecloths that reached the floor and a solitary hibiscus took centre stage on each table lit by a small hurricane lamp. As they took their seats Archie placed his arms royally on the carver chair and was beaming as he turned to the waiter.

'Blimey if we were any closer to the sea, we'd be in it' and laughed at his own joke. Lauren groaned and shook her head.

'My name's Maxwell and I am going to be your waiter this evening.' He began unfolding Alison's napkin and laid it on her lap. He moved around the table. 'Can I get you some water, still or sparking?' In the same way he laid Lauren's napkin across her lap and she immediately snatched it up and placed it on the table again.

'Sparkling please' said Alison noticing Maxwell's greying hair and well worn waistcoat. She decided he had probably encountered more difficult guests than her daughter.

'Yes ma'am and for the young lady?' he turned to Lauren.

'I'll have a rum punch.'

'Wouldn't you rather have wine dear?' Alison glared at her daughter.

'Nope, I'd rather have rum punch.'

'And we do a very good rum punch here. Our barman says it's the nutmeg that makes them so special. I'll get that for you Miss and you sir?' Archie hadn't seemed to notice the exchange between mother and daughter with his head in the menu.

'I had a beer at the bar but I can't remember what it was called and I only had one' he said beaming at the waiter whose kind face had the answer.

'That'll be our Carib beer sir. I'll just get those drinks for you now. Have a nice evening' and he was gone, leaving his diners to bury their heads in the menus. Selecting what to eat was punctuated by Archie with tips he had picked up from reading tourist books in his room. His enthusiasm was halted only by Lauren's look of boredom at each of his suggestions. When the drinks arrived Archie raised his glass in a toast.

'You're to my thoughts as food to life.'

Alison automatically raised her hand to still her daughter knowing all the time she was powerless to succeed.

'What's he on about mum?' Archie wasn't to be stopped, his smile getting wider.

'Gluttony all the way.' He held his glass in the air. Lauren was dumb-struck.

'That's Shakespeare young Lauren.' Lauren rolled her eyes, a move she had perfected, then took out her mobile and began texting furiously.

Alison was well used to Archie experimenting with new ways of occupying himself since he retired. That was the problem with retirement it gave you rather a lot of spare time. He had decided that when it came to 'hanging up his shovel' he would interest himself in things far from his normal line of work. His recent Introduction to Shakespeare class had taken him way outside of his comfort zone but, typical of Archie, he embraced it warmly. So for Alison the fact he might misremember quotes was less important than his passion for something completely new.

Dinner had been more enjoyable than Alison had hoped. Lauren and Archie hadn't come to blows and her daughter had remained at the table throughout the meal. Archie had seen to it that Alison had the best view from the table by seating her facing the sea. She watched the small white lights that were strewn around the balcony as they glittered and tumbled out of sight, then climbed up into palm trees that looked like they had been there since Columbus arrived, giving the whole vista a blanket of glamour. It was all as it should be thought Alison. It was just perfect and then she looked across the table at her daughter who, after four rum punches and two glasses of wine was having some difficulty locating her napkin that had fallen onto the floor. Within seconds Archie was there, trying to help.

'Hang on a minute girl. Archie'll get that for you,' he said as he slid under the table and disappeared out of sight, taking their tablecloth and its contents with him. Alison clung on to her corner as glasses teetered and plates collided. Then, seemingly out of no-where, Maxwell appeared, snatched up the napkin, reorganised the table and took their order for dessert.

As Alison was wondering how she might engage her daughter and distract her from yet another rum punch, ordered in place of dessert, she heard the East coast American voice again, from behind her this time.

'I forget Jack, you're always right about everything. Forgive me but I thought you'd asked for a rail table yet here we are stuck at the back of the restaurant again. You know what, tomorrow I'll book the table myself, how about that?' There was a scraping of a chair across the wooden floor and then another voice, English this time.

'Why don't you just do that?' and suddenly there it was, in amongst the new and unusual, something familiar, something that registered with Alison, it was the English voice. Just a few words but there was something in the tone, in the accent, that made her feel she might know the owner. There wasn't a face that sprang to mind and she didn't feel it would have been right to turn in her seat and stare but something did resonate with her when he spoke. Maxwell had returned to the table and Lauren asked him.

'What's a rail table Maxwell?'

'Keep your voice down Lauren' hissed Alison.

'Well ma'am it's a table in a prime position in the restaurant, like this table you're sitting at now, well this is what people call a rail table. It's considered the best table you can have and it's got a great view of the sea.'

'Without actually being in it' Archie looked hopefully at Maxwell. 'The sea that is' he added. Lauren groaned.

'You've already cracked that gag Archie, give it a rest.'

'Lauren' Alison's voice was sharp and Archie leaned across and put his hand on her arm.

'Don't worry Ali, Archie don't worry about things like that.'

When they turned to leave the restaurant, Alison could see the American woman sitting alone. She smiled and the American smiled back at her but there was no sign of the owner of the English voice.

They drank coffee in the lounge and sat with Joan and Margaret while Lauren took up her position on a stool at the bar. There was a small steel band playing songs from musicals and Alison felt they might all rather be playing something more traditional. Archie was tapping the arm of his chair to *'My heart will go on'* and clearly enjoying himself. The lace from his second shoe had now become undone and was swinging in time to the music. Margaret seemed keen to chat and so Alison took up the role of listener while keeping an eye on Lauren as her bar stool began to sway, although not, in her case, to the music. The bar was quite full now with late diners waiting for a table in the restaurant. The louvered shutters were all pushed open along the length of the room allowing the breeze to slide through. Alison began to feel tired but she was so enjoying the moment she wanted to stay listening to the band with the breeze against the back of her neck. Of course such blissful moments are often shattered and so it was for Alison, as Lauren fell backwards off her stool into the lap of an elderly gentleman enjoying a pre-dinner drink with his wife.

Back in the room Alison chose to sit on the balcony while Lauren used the bathroom. She had no idea the acoustics were so good. Perhaps she would sleep on the balcony. It was filled with furniture: a small sofa with large cushions, faded from the sun, a corner table and lamp and a table for breakfast. There was a picture on the wall of a beach, perhaps this beach. Tomorrow she would find out. Lauren appeared at the balcony door.

'That rum punch is lethal,' said Lauren slumping onto the sofa. Alison smiled in sympathy.

'That'll be the nutmeg I expect.'

TWO

It hadn't been the best night's sleep Alison had ever enjoyed although Lauren slept soundly from the moment her head touched the pillow. She was still sleeping as Alison went out onto the balcony just as the sun was coming up.

Falling in love with Nevis had been a swift decision for Alison. She had read somewhere that your favourite Caribbean island was always the first one you ever visit and so, she decided, it was inevitable she would love it here. The boat that brought them from St Kitts had been full of locals returning to Nevis and Archie engaged them all in conversation as Alison let the wind and spray blow through her hair and Lauren sat inside listening to her iPod. It was the greenness of the island that had stunned her as they approached. She always imagined Caribbean islands to be dry and dusty but all she could see were twelve thousand acres of forest coming into view.

Alison wrapped her dressing gown around her, gazed into the distance and enjoyed her first ever Caribbean morning. The sky was clear except for the odd rogue cloud that came into view and was quickly blown out of sight. The only noise to be heard was chattering birds. Over the balcony she could see into the next building and so far there wasn't any sign of Archie. The guest bedrooms were scattered around the garden in groups of two, ground and first floor and Lauren had been delighted with their first floor room. She had been even more delighted to find that Archie wasn't sleeping downstairs in their block, not wishing to, in her words, 'wake in the middle of the night and imagine myself lying face down on top of bloody Archie'. Alison however would have quite liked to be lying face down on top of Archie but it was he who had insisted she share a room with Lauren so her daughter wouldn't be made to feel uncomfortable. Whereas Lauren was making it her life's work to ensure Archie was made to feel 'uncomfortable'. Alison accepted their relationship was going to take some work and truly hoped Archie's idea of this holiday would help.

There was movement across the gardens. Archie's patio doors opened and for a moment she watched the man who had become such an important part of her life. He was already dressed in vivid green and yellow shorts with a collared shirt that was, for the moment, tucked into his shorts. His boat shoes looked new, as did everything else, and he was smoothing back his hair at the sides and then carefully patting the top of his head where the hair was less evident. He took a map out of his back pocket and laid it on the table. He was planning what they might do today. Just as Alison was about to call out she heard the patio doors downstairs open and the American woman's voice carry outside. It was difficult to make out what was being said but Alison decided it sounded congenial enough and that the disagreement at dinner last night must have been forgotten. Then she recalled the English voice and the strange way in which it was familiar to her. Archie was waving excitedly to get her attention.

'You're up then?' he said and then from behind her Alison heard.

'Does he always have to state the obvious?' Lauren was awake. Alison leaned over the balcony and called to Archie.

'I'll just shower and then perhaps we could have a walk before breakfast?' She heard the doors below snap shut and lowered her voice. 'I'll be there in ten minutes.' Archie waved the map in the air.

'I've got it all planned out. You leave it to Archie' he said beaming.

After showering Alison dressed then brushed her long dark hair back from her face counting what she thought were three more grey hairs than this time yesterday. She leaned into the mirror and decided the time difference was going to prove challenging on this holiday and grabbed her oversized sunglasses.

'You are kidding, mum? You aren't really going to be seen in public with that?' Lauren was on the balcony now and watching as Archie attempted, unsuccessfully, to refold his map and return it to the back pocket of his shorts. Alison coaxed her daughter back into the bedroom.

'Keep your voice down Lauren. He looks perfectly fine. He's on holiday.'

'Mum he looks like a clown in those bright colours. People will expect him to start juggling plates at breakfast.'

As they walked along the beach she yearned to sit in the sand and *feel* where she was. For Alison that was how things had always been. She would *feel* somewhere, that was how she would experience it, not by the doing of it and in that way she and Archie would always be so very different. She closed her eyes and turned her face out towards the sea.

'What are you looking at?' Archie was beside her and she could hear the map rustling in the breeze.

'I'm not looking at anything' she smiled 'my eyes are closed.'

'Well you won't see much that way girl.'

'On the contrary, I can see everything.' More map rustling, 'so what would you like to do today?'

'Me? I've got a list as long as your arm. I'll show you over breakfast.'

Breakfast was taken in a long wooden building right on the beach. Alison sat close to the open window and watched birds dive into the sea and felt the spray on her face. Lauren arrived and Archie held up a menu and waved wildly at her as she came through the door. Then, just as Alison prepared herself for another sarcastic onslaught from her daughter she heard.

'Hey it's really nice here isn't it?' from Lauren.

'There you go Ali I told you she'd like it.' Archie was beaming 'great breakfast menu Lauren, everything from pumpkin pancakes to coconut French toast, what are you going to have?' Uncertain as to how her daughter might react to Archie's familiarity Alison attempted to change the subject.

'You must get lots of lovely mornings like this here?' she asked the waitress who was pouring iced water. The reply was slow and began with a small humming noise that was gentle and accompanied by a wide smile.

'Yes ma'am. Every morning is a beautiful morning on Nevis. This your first visit?' Alison launched into the answer, grateful for the chance to take the focus away from Lauren and Archie.

'Yes first visit, in fact first time to the Caribbean.'

'Well then you come to the right place first, you won't want to go no-where else after Nevis. We your family now.'

'Well that was nice' said Alison 'isn't everyone friendly?' Lauren looked embarrassed.

'Mum if you could just stop fawning all over the locals that would be great, try treating them like real people.'

'I'm sorry I didn't realise I was....'

'Being patronising? Well yes you were mum, just a bit.' Pause. 'I'll have the pumpkin pancakes with orange blossom sauce' and she was gone, pulling her mobile out of her back pocket as she left the table. Within seconds she had the phone to her ear and was in conversation before she'd even left the restaurant. Archie looked a little startled by her quick exit.

'She'll be phoning the twins, she missed them last night. It was too late by the time we got here. Bedtime. You know how it is?' But Archie didn't know how it was. He had never married, much less fathered any children. This was all new territory to him. The water-bearer had returned to take their order and a kind of normality was resumed.

Breakfast was busy and Margaret and Joan came in slowly, with Margaret waving enthusiastically at Archie who returned her greeting generously. Both the women were wearing short sleeved blouses with embroidered collars, the younger woman opting for a pale blue and the elderly woman staying safe in navy. They sat close to the door just as Lauren flounced back into the room and announced she'd missed the twins who had already gone to nursery. Alison looked at her watch which still showed the time at home and saw it would be midday in the leafy north London suburb where Lauren's half-brothers lived.

'So you didn't get to talk to the boys?'

Lauren poured the entire jug of orange blossom sauce over her pancakes.

'No and dad's in Stockholm with some clients. The Tooth Pick was there though.' This was Lauren's name for her father's tall, slender, young wife. 'She said to call around five-thirty because the twins have got a music lesson after nursery.'

'Bit young for music lessons aren't they?' Archie looked up from his plate of black beans and bacon, his knife and fork held in mid-air like a conductor waiting to call his band. No-one spoke but Lauren tilted her head to one side, closed her eyes and audibly sighed. After a few moments and getting no response, Archie returned to his breakfast without another word. These were the difficult times when this neatly divided family crossed, albeit temporarily, into each other's ordered lives. When thoughtless comments were passed and closeness assumed, it was the worst of times for Alison.

When Alison thought of capital cities it was Paris, Berlin and Athens that sprang to mind. These were all cities she was familiar with and apart from a short working trip to New York when she was in her twenties, they were places she felt had earned the title, capital city. People would always gravitate towards important cities giving them a real buzz. Now she was driving through Charlestown with not a skyscraper in sight.

'This is the capital' said Archie grinning at her 'I'll let you know when we've passed through it.'

The streets were narrow with deep storm drains that served as a reminder of the ferocious weather the hurricane season could bring. Locals were spilling off the pavement onto the road to pass one another amid tall stone buildings with wooden upper floors and balconies that jutted out over the street. The Government buildings were the grandest of all, in blue and white with outside staircases spiralling to the top and bursting upon round turrets and although most were now rather faded and tired looking they gave the town a feeling of gravitas that registered with Alison. There wasn't a lot of noise, just a general hum of business and laughter, the kind of laughter that's missing from most serious cities.

'Archie I love it. I can't tell you why it's just the feel of the place.'

'You got your eyes closed again girl?' he joked as he parked the car alongside the History Museum. 'I wish Lauren had come along, I thought this might be right up her street.' Alison couldn't share with Archie that Lauren hated museums. She saw them as a selective approach to any form of history and would refuse to go through the door of even the most prestigious building. Although things might have been different today thought Alison as she walked into an area only slightly bigger than her living room and watched as Archie collected all available brochures and books so that 'the girl won't feel left out' but Alison knew that being 'left out' is exactly where Lauren wanted to be.

Back at the hotel they found Lauren on the beach, completely disinterested in where they had been or what they had done although she did promise to look at the books Archie had brought back. When he disappeared to change, Alison sat down beside her daughter who was now ready to talk.

'You missed all the excitement this morning, there was a massive row going on downstairs after you left.' Lauren turned over tossing the sun lotion to her mother. 'I mean what's the point of people going on holiday together when all they do is row?' Alison smiled at the irony of her daughter's statement. 'She really had a go at him this morning. Would you cream my back mum please?'

'He's English I think. You really shouldn't eavesdrop like that Lauren.' Lauren squirmed as Alison squirted the cream on the small of her back.

'Oh right like you don't want to know.'

'I don't, really I don't. It's just that I thought his voice was vaguely familiar when I heard it last night at dinner. I don't suppose it meant anything to you did it?'

'Me?' Lauren turned over to face her mother 'last night's dinner is a bit of a blur to be honest.'

'And you didn't recognise his voice this morning then?'

'No can't say I did although they were in yelling mode most of the time, she was so pissed off with him, you could tell, really pissed off.'

'Who's that then?' Archie had returned wearing a pair of swimming shorts that Alison thought might have benefited from being a size larger. They were navy with a lively orange design and still had the shop label attached at the back.

'Just the couple in the room downstairs, they don't seem to be getting along very well, Lauren heard them arguing this morning.'

'Probably jet-lag' said Archie 'they say it can make people grumpy, although we seem to be alright don't we?' He wore his genuine smile and Lauren groaned loudly.

'Great swimmies Archie' she said not making any attempt to stifle her giggle, 'they must be new?'

'Yes, I really enjoyed shopping for this holiday' he was beaming 'I thought they were very suitable but I'm not sure what these orange things are' he said pulling the shorts to one side.

'They're surf boards Archie. Planning on doing a bit of surfing are you? Let me know if you do 'cause I wouldn't want to miss that.'

'Well if Archie decides to take the plunge you'll be the first to know young Lauren. I'll get us a couple of sun beds in the shade, don't want to rush things on our first day do we'. Alison leant across to her daughter.

'That was really unkind and quite unnecessary.'

'For Christ's sake mum the bloke talks about himself in the third person, I just can't take him seriously.'

'Well I'd like you to try, even if it's just for my sake. I'm off to get changed for the beach now and please when I get back could you just try a little harder.'

The room had been serviced and fresh flowers left in the bathroom where yellows and blues, purples and red were all crammed into a small glass vase with no great arrangement other than the practiced hand of the girl who picked them. Alison had watched her earlier, pulling the best of the blooms from amongst the hedging knowing that by this time tomorrow they would all have been replaced with flowers of equal beauty. She studied the vase and whilst she knew that purple and red were not usually companion colours, in this place they worked, in this sunny and brilliantly lit island, these colours could reside alongside one another and look just perfect. She stopped and without thinking adjusted a painting on the wall to bring it into line, it was a habit of hers, learned long ago and never able to be forgotten.

Looking at her reflection in the mirror Alison took two brown hair combs and pushed her hair up onto the top of her head and secured it in place. She had caught the sun on her face and as she applied protection she pulled her skin back from her face losing about ten years in the process. It was an effect she approved of. She tried to decide if she was brave enough to use only a sarong to cover her swimsuit on her way to the beach or whether she should slip on a skirt and t-shirt. The black swimsuit was new, to match her new slimmer body, a side effect of an unhappy divorce. The days of Robert and month long summer holidays in a French farmhouse eating and drinking their way through each day were a thing of the past. She grabbed the sarong and pushed it into her beach bag, then pulled on her skirt and t-shirt and left the room.

Halfway down the stairs she heard voices and a door closing in the downstairs room, she held back and decided to let her warring neighbours go first in case they were mid-way through yet another argument. She had made the right decision.

'Oh excuse me' the American woman was saying 'I thought this holiday was supposed to be a celebration for my birthday.'

'Isn't everything always centred round you?' he was almost shouting.

'You know what if you're gonna yell at me I think I'd rather spend the day on my own.' She was walking away from the room now in a long, flowing kaftan and Alison recognised the short cropped haircut as the woman from dinner last night.

'Don't be ridiculous, you can't be on your own today, it's your birthday for Christ's sake.' She noticed how the English accent had been warmed by the American dialect and finally the owner registered with her. 'Wait will you, we'll walk together.' She heard the door slam shut and ran downstairs just in time to see him walk across the gardens towards the woman who had decided not to wait. Alison stood at the corner of the building and watched this tall slender man with dark grey hair, long enough to just cover the collar on his polo shirt, take long lazy strides away from her, just as he had done over thirty years ago. Then she sat down on the stairs, put her head in her hands and began to cry.

THREE

Absenting herself from the beach had been easy for Alison through a series of brief text messages that complained of jet-lag, too much sun and a headache. She was grateful for Archie's maleness in that he didn't press her for details. The maddening thing was she didn't truly understand why it was she had begun to cry but rather put it down to shock that now, after all this time, they had come face to face. Although it wasn't strictly true that they had come face to face, Alison had only seen him walking away from her, but she knew absolutely that it was John, her John.

Lauren's plan to stay on the beach all day working on her suntan hadn't, of course, included Archie but he seemed happy to spend the afternoon planning their next outing from his patio. From her balcony Alison could hear him moving around outside and the occasional fizz-pop as he took the ring pull off a can. Then there would be the passing word for a cleaner or gardener, nothing of any great value, just a word or two almost as though he couldn't let them pass without connecting with them in some way. Alone and yet never alone, that was Archie.

It can be exhausting spending the whole afternoon dwelling on the past, on the hurt, on what might have been but at the end of it the only thing Alison had resolved was that Archie could never know about John. Somehow she would have to keep it hidden from this dear man who had looked forward to the adventure of this holiday for weeks and was still hoping to win over her daughter. Outside she could hear he was trying to engage with another passer-by, it was Lauren and Alison feared it may not turn out well.

'Glad I've seen you' Alison thought she heard an audible groan from Lauren, 'come here and have a look at this, tell me what you think.'

'Sorry Archie I'm just on my way to the room.'

'That's alright, won't take a minute' there was the flapping of a map in the breeze and Alison moved towards the corner of the balcony hoping she could rescue things should Lauren launch into one of her attacks on this unsuspecting victim. 'Look at this place here' he was circling an area inland on the map.

'Well to be honest Archie it doesn't mean a thing, I mean it's a map, you've heard about women and maps, we don't understand them do we?' It was easy for Alison to read the subtext in Lauren's speech but Archie carried on completely unaware of her sarcasm.

'Let me show you in the travel book then' he was searching amongst a pile of books on his patio table and Alison didn't have to be standing next to them to know Lauren's patience was running out. 'Here it is,' she breathed a sigh of relief. 'I wondered what you might think of this, you being interested in history.'

'Okay' big sigh 'what is it?'

'They say this is the oldest house in the whole of the Caribbean' he said triumphantly.

'Who are they?'

'The person who wrote the book I suppose' Archie was caught off-guard by the request for detail but moved on fearlessly 'but look we can go and see it, even have tea in it. Supposed to date back to 1680, they call it' he screwed up his eyes and moved the book closer, 'a plantation house. Sounds just up your street I would have thought, what do you think?' There followed a long pause.

'So you really want to know what I think?' Alison began to panic and Lauren went on 'I'll tell you what I think. I think 1680 is around the time the British were increasing their traffic of Africans to America and the Caribbean for the slave trade and I think the people who were living in this plantation house were almost certainly living off the proceeds of slavery.'

'Hey steady on girl' Archie was lowering his voice 'not everyone round here might want to hear talk like that.'

'You mean the locals?' more sarcasm, 'you think they don't know, you think three hundred years of persecution might have passed them by?' Lauren was really getting into her stride now, 'or perhaps you think they'd rather not talk about it, brush it under the carpet and pretend it was all a figment of their imagination?'

When she arrived back in the room Lauren was red-faced but not from the heat of the sun.

'That bloke is about as sensitive as a flying hammer.'

'Why do you do it Lauren, what makes you bully that poor man so?'

'You won't like it.'

'I'd still like to know.'

'Because I think he's stupid if you must know. I think he's stupid and clumsy and awkward and' Lauren was searching for words now.

'And working class?' said Alison quietly.

'It's got nothing to do with that' she snapped. 'Look he could be completely fucking class-*less* and I'd still think he wasn't good enough for my mother.' Alison was shaking her head. 'I don't want to talk about this anymore mum. I hate the fact we're here but we are and there's nothing I can do about it but to be honest I just don't know where all this is going to end with me and him.' She started taking out her text books and throwing them on the bed. 'Anyway are you feeling any better now? Bit sudden your 'jet-lag' wasn't it? I thought you'd probably had enough of him in the morning and needed a break.'

The three of them walked down to dinner that evening, not together exactly and not trying to look like a family, but at least all at the same time. Archie held her hand and Alison clung on to him trying to walk in the shadows, always thinking about John, always afraid he might emerge round the next corner. They sat at the back of the restaurant and she could see John and the American woman sitting at the rail table seemingly deep in conversation. Archie wanted to take coffee in the bar but Alison feigned a headache and he walked her back to her room.

'You'll feel better tomorrow Ali, it's just taking you a while to get used to the time difference.' They were standing outside her room. 'I'll nip back to the bar and make sure Lauren's alright.'

'There's no need Archie, she doesn't need babysitting you know.'

'Archie knows that. I just fancy a drink myself, you don't mind? I could stay if you wanted me to.' Alison didn't want him to stay she just wanted on be her own so that she could think about John.

She sat on the balcony pretending she was listening for Lauren but that wasn't true, more lies. At last she heard John's voice, just before midnight. The American woman was laughing, he had said something to make her laugh and Alison hated it but she stayed there, on the balcony, unable to move away. She imagined them undressing, kissing, holding one another. She remembered how it felt to have him wrapped around her, his face buried in her neck, his strong arms pulling at her clothes. Then she wept for an affair that had never finished, just paused, all those years ago in the middle of the night when the phone call came, to say it was over.

Lauren arrived back in the room much less drunk than she had been the night before and desperate to talk. These were the delightful times when being Lauren's mother was a joy.

'So what that means is that none of the locals cooks on Friday or Saturday nights on Nevis. Romeo says the women go on strike and all the families eat out at the local barbeques.' She was shouting from the bathroom. 'Of course I challenged him on why the cooking was only down to the women but he wouldn't be drawn. Anyway, he said that he'll take me this week so I can get a flavour of the local culture.'

'And Romeo is?' Lauren came back into the room and sat on the edge of her mother's bed brushing her long copper coloured hair.

'Maxwell's son. You know Maxwell, he was our waiter at dinner last night and Romeo works behind the bar. I got chatting to him last night but to be honest I can't really remember what we talked about but I think he was the one who picked me up after I fell off that bar stool.' Alison blushed on her daughter's behalf at the very thought of it.

'Did Archie come back and find you?'

'God yes but I managed to shake him off. He was chatting to those two women he introduced us to last night before dinner. He does go into some detail mum, going on about buildings and things and deliberating over the usefulness of sash windows. Shit he's boring.' She threw the hairbrush in the direction of her, as yet still unpacked, suitcase and got into bed.

'He's a builder Lauren, well an ex-builder. He's interested in stuff like that, it was his bread and butter once upon a time.'

'And that just goes to show how fucking boring he really is then doesn't it? Anyway the younger one, is her name Margaret? She was hanging on his every word. I think you might have a bit of competition there mum. Oh and Romeo says they have a Calypso evening here every Thursday and the place really rocks.'

'Thursday? That's tomorrow then.'

'Yes. It's down on the beach and he works the bar. It's always a really good night apparently. So I guess we'll be going, as long as Archie doesn't have any trips organised for us.' Lauren started to yawn.

'I'll make sure of it.' Alison smiled.

'I almost forgot he has got something planned. He said to tell you you're playing golf tomorrow. He'll let you know what time you kick-off in the morning.'

'I think you mean tee-off.'

'Right' more yawning, 'you sound a lot better tonight.'

'I think it's you that's a lot better tonight my darling,' but Lauren was already asleep.

Alison awoke early with the John-problem at the front of her mind. She looked across at her half-sleeping daughter who had come back in good spirits last night and used only two expletives to express her dislike of Archie. Alison saw this as progress.

A note had been pushed under the door. It was from Archie and it was brief. Their tee-time was 10.15 and he would see her at the golf club. Alison continued reading the note out loud to Lauren.

'Archie says if I'm not up to it he's sure you won't mind driving the buggy for him today. Perhaps you'd like to come along?'

'One thing's for sure mum, you had better feel up to it because I'm not driving Mr Boring around all day in a golf buggy. No way.'

'And I thought you were softening towards Archie.'

'You should stop talking in code mum' said Lauren turning over in bed. 'Anyway, I've got a lot of catching up to do work-wise today. You go. I didn't know you liked golf that much?'

'I don't, but I'll enjoy driving the buggy. Yes actually, I quite fancy that today.'

Although she wasn't going along to play, Lauren insisted on accompanying her mother to the golf club to, 'see what Archie's come as today'. Archie had spent a long time shopping for clothes for the holiday and Alison knew it had given him a lot of pleasure, although she was sometimes mystified at his choices. She secretly believed that the vivid colours and loud designs didn't work quite as well on him as he thought they did and Lauren just thought he looked comical, no matter what he wore.

'If he's wearing anything like those swimmies he had on yesterday this could be hilarious' whispered Lauren as they rounded the corner towards the shop. Then they saw him, in front of a long mirror, making final adjustments to his appearance. Lauren could barely contain herself. 'It's too late to take them back I suppose?' she called out nudging her mother who felt Archie might have needed a little help in coordinating his outfit. The shorts were a mass of brilliantly coloured zigzags, kept in place by a dazzling silver belt and whilst his polo shirt was more conservative, the lime green simply did nothing for either Archie or the shorts. The golf shoes were at least a simple brown and white for which Alison was thankful.

'What do you mean young Lauren? I'll have you know these are Captain Thunderbolt shorts' he said beaming.

'They certainly are' laughed Lauren.

'Who's Captain Thunderbolt?' asked Alison.

'He's an Australian convict who escaped from Cockatoo Island,' replied Lauren.

'Oh dear. Is he still at large?'

'Alive and well and living on Nevis by the look of it,' said Lauren nodding at Archie who was now trying on a variety of caps to complement his outfit. 'I like the pink one Archie' shouted Lauren. Her mother threw her a fierce glance.

'No not the pink. How about the beige? That would probably work better' said Alison taking control as she waved her daughter away from the shop. 'We should go now Archie. It's nearly our tee time.'

Outside Alison took the driving seat as Archie ordered lunch for the ninth tee and then they drove the cart quickly round to the tee box. Archie was first out of the buggy and gestured towards Alison.

'Come and meet our golfing partners Ali, this is Milva.' A woman with short strawberry blonde hair walked towards her smiling broadly, 'and her husband Jack. They're staying here. In fact, they've got the room downstairs from yours.'

FOUR

They were face to face. 'We spoke in the bar last night' Archie was saying. 'I'd seen them yesterday afternoon while I was on my patio, sunning myself,' he laughed, and Alison secretly hoped he didn't have his shirt off at the time. 'So I suggested we pair up this morning. Nice to have a bit of company.'

'Hi', Milva's hand was outstretched and her smile was warm. Alison had recognised the name immediately. Gathering her thoughts, she said how much she was looking forward to the game, that she wasn't a golfer but enjoyed driving the buggy for Archie but what she didn't say was *oh and by the way I've slept with your husband but you were only engaged at the time so that's alright isn't it?* John had removed his sunglasses and Alison was without words.

'John Houlihan' he said holding out a hand. Alison shook it and didn't want to let go. Milva was laughing at him.

'Hey, that's a bit formal "John Houlihan"'. She put her arm around his shoulders. She was slightly taller than him. 'He's Jack. Only the British could make a formality out of saying 'hi'.' Alison knew she must have looked taken aback. 'Oh don't mind me, sweetie. Jack still can't work me out and we've been married almost thirty five years, which means I've got a coral anniversary gift to look forward to, I think.' He pulled away from his wife and she turned towards Alison. 'Actually honey, I'm planning on hanging on in there until we get to forty, that's ruby. Now there's a precious stone worth waiting for.' She laughed and walked across to the tee. Archie was already there and sizing up his shot, with lots of knee bending and casting of grass into the wind. Then he returned to the buggy, selected a wood and stood to one side waiting for John was standing next to her now, so close she could feel his arm on hers and the warmth of his body. She looked straight ahead without speaking. He leaned towards her and whispered.

'Look I suggest we keep this just between the two of us.' There he was making all the decisions again and for a moment she became irritated with him and angry because he could still make her feel that way. Her face began to flush and she panicked at the thought that Milva might know her name. She had always wondered how much John had been able to keep from his fiancee but then there was so much Alison didn't know.

John looked up and nodded towards Archie telling him to take. Archie moved to the tee with Milva looking on. The club hit the ball with a crack and kept a straight line down the fairway and Milva gave praise.

'Nice shot Archie.'

John moved away to take his place on the tee and then turned back to Alison and leaned in towards her. 'You're looking very good by the way.'

Alison watched as the man she had adored all those years ago steadied himself and almost elegantly, she thought, drove the ball down the fairway. Milva walked passed him towards the ladies tee without a glance in his direction. What a waste thought Alison, to be married to such a beautiful man and not take the time to enjoy him.

It didn't take long before Archie was announcing himself as 'the world's worst player' and blaming the borrowed clubs.

'I wanted to bring mine along Jack but these girls had so much luggage I had to leave them at home. Got to give in to them though haven't we, although goodness knows what they've got in their cases, eh?' He turned to Milva, 'what do you pack Milva? I think Ali brings the kitchen sink.' Alison squirmed and felt embarrassed at his familiarity with her ex-lover and his wife. Although if she was being truthful she would have admitted she squirmed because he was embarrassing her, making her feel like a little woman, his little woman and she didn't want that, not here in front of John. She wanted to appear aloof and independent, remote and self-ruling but instead she felt small and in the way.

Behind the second tee there was a derelict Sugar Mill and Alison wandered over to get some shade while the golfers took their shots. The grey stones were cold to the touch and covered in pale blue flowers. She ducked down and went through a small cave-like entrance and was engulfed in the cold, dark air. She felt a hand on her arm and turned to find that John had followed her in. He pulled her towards him.

'Take care. The ground's very uneven in there and you can't see a thing.'

'I'm fine' she said realising those were the first words she had said to him since they had met and she wasn't sure how 'I'm fine' might qualify as the right thing to say after all this time.

'I see Alison has become Ali now' he said smiling. He still held her arm and she stood completely still so there was no reason for him to remove it. 'I must admit this is one big surprise. I never thought I'd see you again.' He was gripping her more tightly now, 'I never got the chance to explain. Michael said you were very upset.' For a second she switched her thoughts to Michael, one of the kindest men she had ever met. Jack was pulling her closer to him now 'I had no choice, you do realise that don't you? I had no choice.' Alison searched for words but none came so she peeled his hand off her arm and walked back to the buggy.

Milva and Archie were enjoying their new friendship and compared shots while the American did a sterling job managing Archie's exuberance. All the while John distanced himself from them in an almost superior way and continued to beat them shot for shot. Alison couldn't take her eyes off him, the way his hair fell over his face when he leant over to take a shot, his bronzed profile and those dark blue eyes, the colour of the ocean, that she could never forget. She watched every move he made, the way he wrapped his long slender fingers around the club, the way he swayed into a shot. She had always thought he was the most perfect man she had ever seen and now, even after all these years, even when she was desperate to change her mind, she couldn't. He was John and to her he was perfect.

Relief came when the lunch buggy arrived with stuffed sandwiches and cold drinks which they ate as they travelled, trying to avoid a few stray cows that had wandered onto the fairway. Archie attacked his food with his usual gusto and managed to drip the mustard mayonnaise down the front of his lime green shirt creating a Jackson Pollock Scratch Project.

By the eleventh hole the wind had got up and Alison stood back and took in the view of neighbouring St Kitts. Apart from her 'I'm fine' delivered at the Sugar Mill she realised she hadn't had any direct conversations with John and wondered if either Milva or Archie might have noticed this.

'That's some view, huh?' Milva was beside her looking out towards St Kitts. 'I love this place' she said looking around.

'You've been here before?'

'No. First time but straight off I just loved it.'

'How funny' said Alison. 'That's exactly how I felt.'

'You a first-timer too?'

'Yes, we both are. Well this holiday is Archie's treat to be honest. He sold his building company last year and wanted us all to have a special holiday.'

'*Us all*, you say? So not just you and Archie here then?'

'No my daughter, from a previous marriage, is with us.'

'So you married to Archie now then?'

'Oh no' Alison began to falter. 'Sorry I'm not making myself very clear am I?' she laughed and thought she was sounding nervous. 'No, I'm divorced and Archie and I are, well we are...'

'Having a thing?' She had raised one of her eyebrows, which Alison thought very clever, and was half smiling.

'No, it's more than that' she said feeling embarrassed.

'More than *a thing*? Hey that's serious.' Milva laughed. 'I think I get what you mean. He's a nice guy.' She looked across to the tee and shouted as Archie sent his ball off down the fairway. 'There's a shot! Gotta go, try and beat these guys.' Alison watched as she walked away and thought how much she liked her and what easy company she was but couldn't help wonder just how much Milva knew about her existence all those years ago. Did she know her by name, did she know she was English? How much had John told her?

The game was over and Alison hung around outside the clubhouse while they all changed their shoes. Archie was out first and he took her hand as they walked up towards the bar. He'd replaced the 'Jackson Pollock-look' polo shirt. Alison liked him better without food all down his front. When Milva and John arrived there was tension between them and they both looked a little strained but Archie clearly hadn't picked up on any of this and bowled straight into the conversation.

'Do you just let him win Milva or is he really better than you?' Alison's stomach hit the floor. 'I think you let him get away with it.' He turned to Alison. 'What do you think Ali? How much do you think she lets him get away with?' She felt her face turn scarlet at the question.

'You hot in here?' asked Milva. 'It is hot. I don't think they've got the air con working properly. Why don't we take our drinks outside, there's a breeze out there.' She turned to her husband. 'I'll have a Jack Daniels.'

'Bit early for that isn't it?'

'I don't think so, do you Jack?' This time there was no missing the atmosphere, even for Archie, who promptly took Alison's arm and led her away.

Outside they were greeted by much waving from Margaret who, having left her mother in the shade was on the lookout for company. As they approached she eagerly latched on to Archie. Alison made a bee-line for the shade where she found the elderly woman and noticed both she and her daughter were, yet again, in matching outfits.

'You look nice and cool,' lied Alison as she sat down beside Joan who was awkwardly applying a noisy hand-held fan to the back of her neck. 'Can I do that for you?' Joan handed over the fan without a moment's hesitation or gratitude.

'Usually I can rely on Margaret to be on hand for these sorts of jobs but she seems to be regularly taking her leave from me this holiday.' She nodded towards her daughter who was now deep in conversation with Archie.

'Are you having a nice time?' asked Alison who was practiced at moving things in another direction.

'It's a real nuisance you know, I need to be able to rely on someone and surely a mother should be able to rely on her daughter? Is that asking too much?' She pierced Alison with two small eyes both clouded with cataracts. 'You have a daughter don't you?'

'Yes. Just the one.'

'Well you only need one if they behave themselves.' Alison couldn't help herself and laughed out loud at the very thought of Lauren behaving herself.

'I'm not sure how I feel about women behaving themselves.' Milva had joined them. Joan shot her a glance that might have killed a man at a hundred yards.

'You're American?' it was an accusation.

'You've guessed.'

'And do you have children?' asked Joan.

'Not something we ever got round to.' It was an answer that Alison felt was supposed to put an end to the subject.

'Well then you wouldn't know. Never mind, things will improve when we get home and I move in with Margaret. Now if you'll excuse me I'm going to have to tear my daughter away from your', she looked at Alison, 'I forget, is he your husband?'

'Not my husband, no.' Joan took a stick in each hand and leaned into them.

'Well it wouldn't make a lot of difference to Margaret if he was.' Then in a lower voice, 'she's not very choosey, if you get my drift?' and with that she made off in the direction of her daughter.

Milva exhaled loudly, 'She really is something but, hey, it's her daughter I feel sorry for. Which one is she?'

'Over there with Archie.' Alison looked around but couldn't see them. Archie and Margaret had disappeared. Just then Joan turned to look at her and, almost triumphantly, lifted one of her walking sticks and waved it in the air as if to underline their disappearance.

'What do you suppose that means?' asked Milva.

'I don't know but I think she's very odd.'

'And I think you're very polite.'

FIVE

Lauren was meeting them in the beach bar for a drink before the Calypso Evening. She'd gone early to chat with Romeo who seemed to be making quite an impression on her and Alison and Archie were taking their time in joining her.

'I meant to ask' said Alison 'where did you get to this afternoon? One minute you were chatting with Margaret and the next you'd both disappeared. I think Joan was a bit cross.'

'I don't know how Margaret puts up with her. She reminds me of my own mother, very demanding, always needing you to be around. Although mother was an angel compared to Joan.' He put his arm around Alison and pointed towards the bar where Lauren could be seen laughing and joking with one of the barmen. 'I think that's Romeo. Lauren spent a lot of time talking to him last night.' The barman was wearing a short sleeved waiter's jacket and his long, braided hair rested easily on his shoulders. Alison could tell her daughter was already quite taken with him and found herself hoping he wasn't going to provide too much of a distraction. Although she had to confess the appearance of Romeo had certainly lightened Lauren's mood over the last twenty-four hours.

'I just telling your daughter she needs to take it easy in the sun. It's very fierce here, it's easy to get burnt.' He was smiling at Archie.

'That isn't my dad, that's Archie.'

'Okay' the word was long, drawn out and slightly embarrassed 'I got that wrong. Sorry Archie.'

'Sorry Lauren you mean. No way he's my dad.'

Alison took time filling her plate at the barbecue, working her way along the line of exotic looking dishes. Each culinary offering was a blaze of colour. From the simplicity of barbecued chicken, golden in a shower of herbs and spices, to prawns and lobster displayed in such a way that rendered them untouchable to Alison: the lobster submissive and the prawns, obedient, all neatly in a row. Alison had spent a long time being obediently submissive. Archie on the other hand took no time at all deliberating over filling his plate and certainly didn't discriminate when it came to selection. His large capable hands steered his dinner plate across the buffet only slowing down to collect some morsel on the way. Lauren joined them at the table and continued her animosity towards Archie. In some ways Alison welcomed this emotional ping pong. It distracted her from the John-problem, which was increasingly becoming the John and Milva-problem as Alison had decided she quite liked the woman. However, just as she was basking in the comfort of her own domestic difficulties Milva and John appeared and squeezed onto the table.

'Bit tight but you don't mind us joining you?' John moved his chair up close to Alison. 'Bit snug over here Archie, any chance you could budge up a bit?'

'I shouldn't think there's any chance of that' growled Lauren glaring at Archie who was about to lead an assault on a whole rack of pork spare ribs and sweetcorn.

'Archie can do that for you Jack, no trouble at all' and he slid his chair in the direction of Lauren who visibly recoiled.

'I like a guy who enjoys his food' said Milva with a sideways glance at her husband who's small fillet of fish sat quietly in the middle of his plate.

The band had started to play, they were loud and energetic and as the volume increased conversation at the table became more difficult. Milva and Lauren engaged head to head and Alison tried to catch the odd word but it was impossible without leaning into John or moving closer to him. Every so often Archie would be drawn in by Milva who had to talk across Lauren to reach her and Alison noticed her daughter sit back in her seat, refusing to contribute until their exchange had finished. She had hoped Lauren might have disguised her dislike of Archie in front of others but clearly that was impossible. Milva was shouting across the table at Alison now.

'Your daughter tells me you worked in New York some years

back, for an art gallery, is that right?' Alison saw John move his plate to one side and get up to leave the table.

'Jack did you hear that, Ali used to work in New York in the seventies.' He sat down again.

'A lot of people did Milva' he was cool as he turned to Alison, 'where were you?'

'I was in Greenwich Village', said Alison telling him something he already knew. 'I can't remember much about it now' she lied.

'Come on mum, you said it was really exciting' Lauren leaned in to Milva, as though they were already good friends. 'There was this massive power cut and mum was left stranded in the middle of the city' she turned to Alison, 'you made it sound way exciting.'

'You don't say, we remember that don't we Jack?' It was said as though she didn't want to remember it and Alison was afraid she knew why.

It had been the last time she had seen John. The last time she had seen or spoken to him. They had been having dinner in the Windows on the World Restaurant on the 107th floor of the World Trade Centre when the power cut happened. The waiters brought in candles and suggested everyone sit tight. She remembered everything: what they ate, where they sat and the way the candlelight revealed the panic in his face. Even when they were plunged into darkness she had felt safe, safe because she was there with him. She watched with sadness as he stopped being her protector and moved into self-preservation mode.

'That night I was in a Broadway show' said Milva 'and suddenly, boom all the lights went out. There'd been this major power outage that had hit all across the city.'

'Broadway, that sounds fantastic, so you're an actress?' Lauren was clearly in love with the idea.

'Not any more sweetie but I was quite a girl in my day.'

'Enough, I don't think this is talk for the dinner table.' John ran his hands through his hair and Alison felt the strain he was under.

'Get real Jack, I'm hardly gonna put the girl off her food now am I?' She turned to Lauren. 'I was in a production called *Oh Calcutta!* you heard of it?'

'God yes' said Lauren very impressed.

'So there we were, well I was only in the chorus but anyway there we were on stage, part way through a scene and out went the lights. The stagehands brought out some flashlights and we tried to carry on but it was impossible. It became so dark we couldn't even find our way to the dressing rooms to pick up our clothes. It can be pretty hazardous backstage. We were all groping around wearing absolutely nothing and then the audience started offering the cast their jackets so we could get outside through the theatre.' She leaned back in her chair to take the applause, still a seasoned performer.

'It must have been chaos.'

'Worse than. The subways were dead, elevators hung in their shafts. There was nothing running, not even water.' She laughed enjoying the story, 'no subway, no taxis, zip. The only light in the street came from the car lights and the problem was we were getting mixed up with the local hookers who were trying to make a living.'

'God weren't you scared?' Lauren was engrossed.

'I guess I must have been' she looked directly at her husband.

Alison remembered looking down on the city that night. It looked like a black cloth had been thrown over it. The service elevator was still working and word was reaching them that they should either stay put or try and get home, right away. She was desperate to stay and watch the candles burn down but she knew that John wanted to go. He wasn't going to risk being found there with her. Not being where he was supposed to be was an integral part of their affair. Alison hated it but was prepared to tolerate most anything just to be near him.

'And what about you Jack, were you in the audience?' Archie was sinking his teeth into the corn on the cob and decorating his face with the yellow kernels at the same time. Lauren threw him a napkin in disgust and, without a word he obligingly tucked it into his collar putting Alison in mind of an Oliver Hardy sketch she had seen as a child.

'Hell no Archie, he was at the game, weren't you Jack?' Alison tried to read Milva's eyes and for a moment. She thought she saw pain and was gripped by the realisation that his wife knew exactly where he was but did she know who he was with? She began to worry this was some bizarre game and all the time Milva knew exactly what she had been to her husband all those years ago.

Alison knew John had said he was watching the New York Mets playing the Chicago Cubs because he'd asked the waiters to let him know the score. It wasn't until days later when she thought over the logistics of getting back from Queens to Broadway in the middle of a power cut that Alison wondered how he might have explained that to Milva. Yet still her only concern was for him and how he might handle the lie. He had left her in a rush and with little ceremony then headed off in the direction of the theatre. His need was always greater than hers. She watched him walk away then turned and walked back to Greenwich Village with a group of students who were going that way.

'They sang along for almost an hour after the lights went out at Shea, didn't they Jack?' She was still fixed on her husband, then suddenly to Lauren, 'but hey at least they weren't on the 86th floor of the Empire State Building, those guys didn't get down until the next day.'

'How cool is that' said Lauren still entranced. 'Mum said there was some serial killer on the loose as well and she ran all the way back to her apartment.'

'Son of Sam' announced Milva 'but they caught up with him just after that.'

'That must have been seriously weird walking around in the pitch black knowing some psychopath could have been hiding in the shadows.'

'Not really' said Alison, 'everyone stuck together and I got home before all the looting started.'

Romeo had arrived at the table encouraging everyone onto the dance floor. Lauren jumped at the chance and Alison breathed a sigh of relief when Milva and Archie decided to follow with Milva taking the lead, striding onto the dance floor, in a stunning trouser suit. There was more space at the table now but Alison left her chair up close to John which gave her an excuse to lean in towards him. This was the man she had adored, a passionate man who would make love to her in the morning and then phone her during the day to say he wanted her again. A young Englishman working at a firm of lawyers in New York, this was the man who had talked of leaving his fiancée so that they might be together. She looked at him now and all she could see was this young man, she wasn't able to see him as he was now, only John as he had been when he was her John, when he belonged to her. His leg was pushed up hard against hers and he pressed his hand down on her thigh as he leant forward to leave the table.

'You did well to survive that' he said, always the master of the understatement.

SIX

Lauren had been right about something, the Calypso Evening did rock, and Romeo returned her to their room after midnight. Alison hadn't intended to eavesdrop on her daughter but she had lain awake for over an hour trying to work out how she might release herself from the joint outing Archie and Milva had planned for tomorrow, which was now today and now she listened as Romeo helped Lauren up off the floor on her way into the bathroom.

'I seem to be making a habit of this' he said. Lauren's reply was accompanied by the toilet flushing followed by the sound of shoes being flung off and her daughter stumbling out of the bathroom and onto her bed.

'You can stay if you like' said Lauren in a theatrical whisper that Alison felt Archie could have probably heard.

'I'll see you tomorrow' came the reply as the door clicked shut.

'Shit' said Lauren dialling a number on her mobile phone and disappearing into the bathroom again as Alison breathed a sigh of relief but her relief was only temporary.

'Dad it's me' pause 'yes I know it's early, I just wanted to talk to you that's all.'

It was a child's voice now, not the voice that had asked Romeo to stay but a little girl needing to talk to her father.

Caribbean mornings are special. They are bright and clear and come upon you slowly, like most things in the Caribbean. They don't suddenly take you by surprise, they more creep up and surround you with their beauty, giving you precious moments to become accustomed to their unique feel. Alison had been sitting on the balcony for some time watching the sun come up and listening to distant sounds: the water breaking on the reef, the small golf carts moving around the resort, a local voice with just a word or two. She didn't need to devote a lot of time or energy to the experience she just allowed it to wash over her as she thought back over the last twenty-four hours. It had been impossible for her to stop thinking about John and how things used to be between them and the guilt became so overwhelming she had left the bedroom, with Lauren sleeping soundly, to lay amongst the cushions on the balcony. A small pebble landed in her lap and she heard a low whistle coming from downstairs. She could see him, his dressing gown pulled tight, his hands pushing through his dishevelled hair.

'I've got to see you' he said 'come down.' Alison didn't move, 'look I know you've been awake for hours, I could hear you moving around', he paused and moved closer to the balcony, 'I can't sleep either. Please come down.'

He was waiting for her at the foot of the stairs and she flung her arms round his neck and he lifted her off the stairs and pressed her up against the wall. Her feet had hardly touched the ground when he pulled her face towards him and began kissing her.

'Mum? Is that you down there?' Lauren was at the bedroom door, half in, half out. Alison pushed John back into the shadows.

'Just getting some air, go back to bed sweetheart', she pulled her dressing gown around her and as she did could feel her heart racing. He was still standing there looking at her when she turned and went back upstairs.

Because she complained of car sickness Lauren had taken the front seat which left Alison in the back with John and Milva. She had gallantly offered in a 'family hold back' way to take the middle seat and allow their guests a little more space. Luckily the drive inland was short although the roads were winding and often unmade as they bumped around like a group of school children in the back of the bus on a day out. Every twist and turn in the road brought him nearer to her and she learned to control her expression as Archie moved the conversation on through the rear view mirror.

'You're going to love this place, especially you Lauren.'

'So you say' said Lauren unimpressed and not looking very much better for having taken prime position in the car.

'It's an old plantation house, the oldest one in the Caribbean you say?' said Milva making Alison wonder why Americans always had to sound so interested in everything.

'Yes, late seventeenth century and it's surrounded by chattel houses. Apparently you can stay in them too, live like the locals eh?'

'I doubt that very much' was Lauren's contribution.

'Well so do I' said Milva 'but I don't suppose it would do any harm to go and have a look huh?' Lauren shifted in her seat 'you're hoping to go on and study history at university, that right?' Alison thought about ploughing in and trying to recover the conversation sensing her daughter's discomfort but decided against it on the basis that this might not be a bad place for Lauren to exercise her learning. 'So what's your problem with all this then?'

'Leave the girl alone Milva' John was sounding irritated 'she's got her own opinions.'

'And I respect that, I'd just like to understand them that's all.' For some reason, unimaginable to Alison, Archie had decided he would answer for Lauren.

'Lauren gets uncomfortable with the fact that it was the proceeds of slavery that built these grand houses.'

'I can speak for myself thank you' said Lauren through clenched teeth.

'I was kinda hoping you might.'

'Right' Lauren half turned in her seat to face Milva, 'I'm just about okay with the tourism thing, it brings a lot of wealth to the island and most people here do work in the industry.'

'So you think it's okay to be here?'

'Yes of course, otherwise I wouldn't be here would I?'

'Okay to be here but we tourists should lock ourselves in our rooms all day then?' Milva was smiling now.

'Obviously not. Look I've studied what happened out here.'

'And in the States' interrupted Milva.

'Yes okay and in the States and the transportation of Africans for slave labour, wherever it took place, is hard for me to stomach. I've not just read it in some tourist brochure I've read the real facts and you end up not feeling great about what happened, even if it was several hundred years ago.'

'But honey most countries have something in their history they might be ashamed of, you can't go hating yourself for ever for the mistakes that were made before you were even born.'

'I realise that' very curt. 'I just don't feel great about it that's all, I don't hate myself for it.'

The plantation house was cool and the ceiling fan rapped a low rhythmic sound over their heads as they walked into the library. The many pictures on the walls reflected the original purpose of the building and large comfortable chairs and sofas littered the rooms. Tea was ordered and served in a very British way out on the patio after which the group split up and wandered through the gardens. Archie and Milva took off to see the chattel houses and Lauren read in the library.

'Alone at last' John was smiling at her 'by the way I think your daughter's timing was just awful this morning. It's been a long time since I've been caught in the act.'

'We weren't.' They were walking deep into garden, making their way over the ancient roots of a large banana tree that blocked the view from the house. He reached out to take her hand and she pulled it away. 'I don't know where all this is going.'

'Yes you do' he said and she thought he sounded irritated with her just as he had done in the car with Milva, 'you want this just as much as I do.'

'How do you know what I want?' She turned to face him. 'Just what's going on here John?'

'I think I'm still in love with you, in fact I don't think I ever stopped being in love with you.'

'But in New York?'

'New York was a mess, I was a mess. I had no choice, it wasn't something I wanted, it was something I had to do. Can't you see that? I made a mistake, I chose the wrong girl. I should have chosen you, I just found out too late.' It was a powerful statement and she was afraid of what she thought was happening. She turned around and walked away from him and just kept walking to put some distance between them so that later she could replay his words in her head and not have to face them being said out loud.

The chattel houses stood out in their sherbet colours in amongst the wooded gardens that were home to the carefully constructed families of monkeys: the old, the parents, the young, the wild. In fact not unlike Alison's own family. When they caught up with Milva and Archie they were wandering around one of the houses and had Lauren with them.

'Look at this Ali there's a hammock on the balcony. I might just slip in there, what do you think Lauren?' threatened Archie.

'I should give it a miss if I were you.' She didn't need to say anything else everyone in the room knew what she meant, everyone except Archie that is who cocked a leg up over the hammock and climbed in. 'Christ' said Lauren turning to leave, however before she got to the door, the hammock had separated from the wall and Archie landed on the floor. 'It's a bit like being responsible for a small child' said Lauren to her mother as she left the house.

It had been difficult to drag Archie away such was his interest in the construction of the buildings. He loved the simple and practical design, the corrugated iron roof and the fact that, if necessary, it was possible to pick up and transport your entire house somewhere else. A concept that Alison decided she would like to apply to her hotel room.

'The monkeys play on the roof at night, they say, why don't we have a couple of nights there Ali?' said Archie on their way back to the hotel, 'you'll come won't you Lauren?'

'No thanks' the answer was abrupt and Archie looked flattened. 'Actually can you pull over I think I'm going to be sick.' Alison got out of the car and stood with her daughter.

'But you're sitting in the front, I don't understand.'

'That's right mum, you don't understand. It's not car sickness I've got, it's Archie-fucking-sickness. Now leave me alone, I'll walk the rest of the way back.'

It was Friday night and Romeo was going to be taking Lauren on a tour of the local village 'Cook-Out' and Alison and Archie were waiting in the bar, trying not to look like responsible parents, until he turned up to collect her. On their way past the restaurant they had watched Joan and Margaret being seated at the very front of the restaurant at a rail table. The candles on the table threw up a glow around them and the glittering lights that had been wound around the rail lit up Margaret's face and Alison saw the girl in her and wondered why she hadn't seen it before.

They had only just sat down and ordered drinks in the bar when Margaret arrived at their table sounding out of breath.

'I'm so glad I've seen you' she was directing her conversation at Archie. 'Mother said you'd been up to the chattel houses today, and I was wondering are they worth the visit?' This confused Alison as the conversation she and Archie had had with Joan earlier had said that, yes indeed they should go, and so it seemed strange Margaret needed confirmation but they gave it anyway assuming the mother and daughter lines of communication were as unreliable in their household as they were in Alison's.

'It's just with mother having difficulty walking I wasn't sure, I expect we could get a taxi.'

'Oh don't you go worrying about that, Archie will give you a lift' said Archie, his smile taking in the whole group. Alison felt Lauren's foot prod the back of her leg, she looked over and saw her daughter raising her eyebrows and nodding towards Margaret. 'You just let me know when you'd like to go and I'll come along, I'd like to see them myself again anyway.'

Alison sat back as Margaret and Archie made plans for the visit and Lauren leant forward.

'Aren't you bothered mum?'

'I think it's very nice he wants to help' Alison replied wondering why she wasn't even a little bit 'bothered' about Margaret's obvious interest in Archie.

When Romeo arrived in the bar he was charming and immediately invited Alison and Archie along too exacting a quick reaction from Lauren.

'They're not interested.'

'Sure they are' said Romeo 'if we take the car we can go around the island and not just go into the village, that way you get to see a bit more of the local culture and you're gonna save your shoe leather girl.' Lauren was silent and Alison fancied the only bit of local culture Lauren was really interested in was Romeo. 'On Nevis we always aks tourists to the Cook-Out.'

'That's very generous of you but I think Archie would rather like to eat here this evening.' It was the best Alison could think of on the spur of the moment but Archie was on it immediately.

'Archie don't care about that Ali. I'll just pop back and get the car keys' and for a moment Alison thought she saw a knowing smile creep over Romeo's face but was really too focused on Lauren's clear annoyance at their joining them.

The Cook-Out was busy with locals enjoying their day off from cooking at home. A large awning was set up and the barbecue heaved under the weight of the spitting chicken and pork. The music had been rigged up with two large speakers hanging off the awning and everyone moved to the music whether they were standing, sitting or just walking around eating, including Archie who ate his way through several helpings of "cookup", a chicken and rice dish, and was then challenged to a game of dominoes by Romeo's grandfather. Alison watched as Lauren's irritation with Archie grew to a new level as he settled in with the locals and Romeo seemed to pick this up too. Almost instinctively he threw his arms around her and Alison heard him say, 'give the man a break', forcing an embarrassed smile out of her daughter.

It wasn't a late evening for Alison and Archie as they were despatched back to the hotel by Lauren who announced that Romeo would be taking her down to the beach to try some of the local drinks and Alison decided her daughter was probably using a euphemism and took no time in leaving. During the drive back to the hotel she struggled with her guilt knowing she had been unable to get her mind off John throughout the evening and Archie's continued efforts to be a caring and considerate partner only made her feel worse. So when they arrived back in the hotel car park and Archie reached across and pulled her towards him she responded passionately and gave an Oscar winning performance that she was later ashamed of.

SEVEN

It was Saturday and in one week this would all be over. This wonderful, generous treat by her loving man, would be history and they could get back home and start again without the distraction of John but for now Alison was faced with the prospect of him being around every corner and of her being unable to stay away from him. She was sure that so long as she kept some distance between them she could cope. There was absolutely no reason for Archie to discover what she and John had once meant to each other, or worse, how he still made her feel when he walked into a room.

'Thing is mum you don't seem bothered at all that Archie's gone off for the afternoon with Tweedledum and Tweedledee.' They were spending time in their room so Lauren could work at her books and so Alison could hide from John. 'I mean can't you see she fancies him? God knows why of course but she's always fussing around him and trying to get to spend time with him. Aren't you bothered?'

'You're reading too much into all that, he's just trying to be helpful that's all.'

'Trying to help himself more like I bet.' Lauren tucked her knees up under her chin as she leaned back amongst the cushions on the balcony. 'Don't get me wrong, I think it's more her than him but she's laying it on a plate for him and let's face it, he can't get many offers.'

It was just starting to get dark when Alison's mobile phone rang, Lauren got there first and threw it across the bedroom at her, 'it's Mr Dull-and-Boring.'

'Sometimes Lauren I wonder if the hospital gave me the right baby when I came home with you'. She answered the phone 'Archie, how's it going?' What followed was a strange conversation during which Alison agreed that it would be fine for Archie to stay overnight at the chattel houses with Margaret and Joan and bring them back in the morning. Joan had fallen in the garden and hurt her ankle and the doctor had suggested they didn't move her for twenty-four hours so a chattel house had been arranged 'complimentary of course' said Archie.

When he insisted he could easily return and go back and pick them up in the morning Alison was puzzled at her own reaction. 'Don't be daft Archie you said you'd like to stay over when we were there but I know Lauren wouldn't want to come and to be honest I wouldn't want to leave her, there have been one or two distractions already and I think she's getting behind with her work. So, I suppose this works perfectly, you stay and enjoy yourself, this is your holiday too you know.' When she finished the phone call she looked at Lauren. 'Well?'

'I don't understand you mum, why the fuck did you do that? It's probably been a plan to get them together, I bet she pushed old bag over or something.'

'And you my dear have an altogether too active imagination. You can get back to your books now, if you like, now you've sorted my life out for me.'

They were in the bar when Milva discovered they were without Archie and she insisted Alison and Lauren join them at their table.

'We've got a rail table this evening, plenty of room for all of us. Jack can arrange it.'

'Is a rail table important then?' asked Lauren mischievously.

'It is to me' said Milva, 'I like the view over the ocean and if it's a clear evening you get a good view of the stars. It's the best seat in the restaurant and I like to eat there.'

'But doesn't everyone want to sit there?'

'I guess so but it's about who books it first.'

'Or who gives the biggest tip' said John.

'Don't listen to him' said Milva 'they're not like that here, I'm sure they make sure all their guests get to enjoy it.' Romeo had brought over their drinks and when he returned to the bar Milva leaned in to Lauren 'so how's it going with the aptly named Romeo, he's a handsome fella?' Alison felt uncomfortable with the questioning but Lauren was entirely happy to tackle things head-on.

'Going great' she sipped her drink 'he's hot isn't he?' Alison almost choked on her martini.

'It's just a little dry' she lied.

'And have you been able to find time to study this week? He must be quite some distraction.' Milva was eyeing up Romeo as he moved around expertly behind the bar, blending in perfectly.

'I think you've done quite well really' said Alison trying to refocus the conversation on work. 'Of course it's important to get to see a bit of the island, I mean I don't know when we will return. Do you think you'll come back?' but Milva was orchestrating her own line of conversation.

'Have you had any discussions with Romeo about slavery?' she looked pointedly at Lauren.

'Hardly' she said, draining her glass and calling over to the bar for a refill.

'Steady Lauren' Alison warned.

'It's only my second mum' she turned to Milva 'last night Romeo got me something called a 'Killer Bee', it was amazing. Honey, passion fruit and rum, of course. Amazing.' Again Milva held course.

'So why not discuss the past with him? You say you feel very strongly about it and here's your opportunity to have a discussion with one of the locals and you don't take it. That confuses me Lauren, I thought you were a bit more ballsy that that.'

'Leave it Milva' John seemed embarrassed by his wife.

'No it's okay' said Lauren 'you're right I suppose but I felt it would be a bit awkward really.'

'Awkward, now there's a great British word, *awkward*.'

'Now your being antagonistic' John looked apologetically at Alison who was, in some ways quite enjoying the exchange between her daughter and the American.

'Not at all, I'm just playing with words, you play with words don't you Jack?' she let the words hang in the air and then she began again. 'Look I don't mean any disrespect here but hell why don't you just come out and say it? Ask him the question kid, it's the only way you'll get any answers.' She knocked back her drink and turned to the group. 'Now let's eat.' It was decided swiftly and as if in shock they all followed Milva into the restaurant like obedient children.

Throughout the meal Alison continued to watch Milva for any hint or suggestion that she might know there had been a connection between her and John all those years ago. There seemed to be plenty of loaded comments but it was making Alison's head buzz trying to file them all away for dissection later. By dessert she felt exhausted trying to second guess this woman and, tired out, she decided to skip the next course, made her excuses and left, leaving Lauren gladly in the company of Milva and John. When she got back to the room she 'phoned Archie who was in the restaurant and promised to call back in an hour. She showered, pulled on her dressing gown and sat in the dark allowing only the light from the garden to illuminate her thoughts as she began her regular post mortem of the evening when there was a tap at the door. It was John.

'Don't do this, I don't want you here. Just go, Lauren could get back any minute. I want you to leave.'

'You and I both know you don't mean that' he said coming into the room and slipping his hands inside her dressing gown. 'Anyway the lovely Lauren is, at this very moment, deep in conversation with my wife over whether the American War of Independence was simply a war between the Americans and the British. Far too high brow for me, I had to make my excuses and leave, now will you just let me hold you.'

'For Christ's sake John, it's too late for this, thirty five years too late. I don't love you any more' she said the words but didn't believe them and he knew that.

'You're lying' he said pushing her down onto the bed, 'we, that's you and me Alison, are still in love. You know it, I know it.' He turned her face to his 'I love you.'

When he kissed her it was as it had been all those years ago, still as tender and loving as it had always been. She kissed his face and his neck then he rolled her over until she was sat across him and looking down at the face she had always been able to conjure up from a distant memory. The moonlight seemed to magically take away all those years in between and he looked like the young man she had loved decades ago and that made her feel like the young woman she had been then.

Her dressing gown slid down over her shoulders and he reached in and pulled her towards him. They were making love. This wasn't just sex Alison decided. This was love as it had been between them so long ago and when she felt him hard inside her she called out just as she had done all those years ago.

She awoke with a start and saw Lauren's bed hadn't been slept in. Stretching out her hand she found John still lying next to her and panic set in when she realised none of it had been a dream.

'Wake up, you've got to go, right now, please John wake up.' He rolled over onto his side and opened his eyes. 'Go now, quickly.' He pulled her down onto the bed and she fought him. 'I'm serious John, I don't know where Lauren is, you've got to go, she could be back any minute and what about Milva?'

'Do you really think she will have missed me?' he shook his head, 'you've got a lot to learn about my marriage.' He dragged himself out of bed and stood at the door. 'I don't want to go. I honestly don't want to go. Last night was just like it used to be between us, nothing was missing and I love you now just as I did then. For me it's just the same Alison and I can't bear the thought of losing you again.' He pulled her towards him. 'We should tell them now, this morning, just get out there and let them know that we're going to be together. Let's do it.' She pushed him away and he stood there with his hair falling over his face, his shoes in his hand and his shirt open to the waist and she thought if he wasn't out of the door in five seconds she might never let him go. Then she thought about Lauren and refocused her thoughts.

'I'm confused John, I just can't work this out now. I need to track Lauren down, go please. We can talk later' and she pushed him out of the room then picked up her mobile and 'phoned her daughter.

EIGHT

The phone rang three times then went to Lauren's answering service. Alison hung up and was trying to sort out the conflicting emotions in her head when the door opened and her daughter came in. The relief she felt at seeing her was immense but as is the way with parents these things often manifest themselves as anger.

'Why the hell didn't you phone?'

'I did.'

'Rubbish Lauren you didn't even bother to let me know you were going to be late.'

'I did call but you didn't pick up, I called four times actually mum.'

'That can't be' said Alison 'unless there's something wrong with my phone.' Lauren leaned over and picked up her mother's mobile.

'It's on silent and you've got seven missed calls' she threw the phone back onto the bed 'four from me and three from Archie, looks like he gave up on you.' Alison grabbed the phone and scrolled through the messages, remembering that she had turned her mobile to silent so she wouldn't have to take Archie's call while John was there with her. She wasn't used to such devious behaviour.

'I'm sorry, I just didn't know you were going to be this late.'

'I wasn't' there was silence. 'I wasn't that long after you.'

'Why didn't you wake me up?'

'You weren't asleep' said her daughter fixing her with a hard stare.

'But I didn't hear you come in.'

'I'm not surprised and anyway you had your back to the door.'

'Jesus Christ Lauren, what are you saying?' The gloves were about to come off.

'Do you make a habit of this sort of thing mum? This is the second time I've walked in on you and some bloke and I've got to tell you, it doesn't get any easier.'

'Oh god, how awful.' Alison felt the blood rush to her cheeks, 'I'm so sorry you had to witness that, truly I am.'

'So, the fuck, am I.'

'Language Lauren.'

'Christ mum don't have a go at me about my language when you're spending your time screwing around. Did you and Jack plan this, I mean what about Archie I thought you really liked him, you spend all your time telling me you like him and what a nice bloke he is and the moment he's off doing something else you're shagging the guy downstairs. I just don't get it.'

'I know, poor Archie' said Alison and she really thought that, poor decent Archie.

'Hey even I'm thinking poor Archie and I can't stick the bloke and that's not normal for me mum, feeling sorry for Archie, it's not right.'

'Look sweetheart I need to tell you something so you'll understand' she paused to briefly consider how she might phrase what she wanted to say but finding it far too difficult she just ploughed on, 'but that wasn't the first time with John I mean Jack.' Alison immediately knew she could have constructed it better.

'Jesus mum how many are there? John *and* Jack?'

'No, they're the same person.'

'Thank fuck for that. How long have you been at it?'

'That was the first time this holiday' Lauren didn't look much relieved, 'what I mean is I first knew John many years ago.'

'Oh don't tell me it's *complicated*' she said mocking her mother.

'Not really. We met just after I left Art School and went to work in New York. I knew him as John then, he was a lawyer and had come over from his London office to work for their New York firm. He was flatting with his cousin Michael, a lovely Irishman and he introduced us.'

'So you knew his cousin first?'

'Yes he's a firefighter and we met when he came to check out the gallery.'

'So did you date him first?'

'Sort of, well yes actually I did, but nothing very serious and once I met John well that was it, love at first sight and all that.

'I think I'm going to be sick' said Lauren. 'So John nicked you off his cousin, nice bloke.'

'You make it sound really seedy and it wasn't like that, they were really close and anyway Michael fell in love himself after that with someone from John's office. John used to tease me saying she looked so much like me he was looking for my double but I know that wasn't true, they were so much in love, you could see it.'

'Oh good I'm glad it had a happy ending' said Lauren sarcastically. 'So go on, I mean if you were so in love why didn't you get married?' Alison hesitated.

'Well, he was already engaged to someone else' she checked for her daughter's reaction, 'now I know that might sound awful but I don't think either of us thought we were going to fall in love when we met.'

'Oh well that's alright' more sarcasm, 'so he dumped you then?' Alison hated the expression.

'If you want to put it like that I suppose. In fact it was Michael who phoned me to call it off.' Lauren was astonished.

'Hang on mum, you're having this brilliant love affair and then he gets his cousin to dump you, what a great bloke' she was laughing now. 'I can't believe you even want to speak to him again let alone shag him for Christ's sake, I mean he couldn't even finish it himself?'

'It was...' she hesitated.

'Don't you dare say *complicated*.'

'Look he was engaged to one of the partners' daughters at the law firm where he worked, there was a date set for the wedding and she found out he was having an affair. Apparently the balloon went up, well that was how Michael put it, and he was forced to make a choice.'

'And he chose her?'

'Yes. I didn't have any communication with him at all after that. Michael said it had to stop immediately otherwise he might lose his job. I was young and I suppose I didn't want any trouble, for him or me. I was a bit out of my depth to be honest.'

'Did you know her?'

'No' more hesitation, 'but I do now.'

'Oh fuck, it's Milva' Lauren was caught between a laugh and a scream, 'I walked back with her last night from the bar, I really like her mum, she's really nice.'

'Oh god Lauren, I like her too, please stop.'

'So while she was letting herself into her room downstairs you were up here getting it on with her husband.'

'You're not making this very easy Lauren.'

'I'm your daughter, I'm not supposed to make things easy for you am I?' There was a long pause as though she was thinking it through. 'So when was the last time you saw him?'

'July '77 the evening of the power cut in New York.' Alison would never say it out loud but last night she had taken back the years and remembered how things had once been between them. John was right when he said it felt the same, it had and she longed to feel like that again, young, vibrant and in love.

'I get it now, no wonder you didn't want to talk about it the other night in front of Milva. I wonder how much she knows?' That was the question Alison would dearly love to have answered but in truth she simply didn't know.

When they were in bed and trying to sleep Lauren asked her if she loved him and she said she did, then Lauren asked her if she loved Archie and Alison said the thing that she most hated hearing people say, she said she, 'was very fond of him' and Lauren said, as she went off to sleep, 'that's a cop-out mum' and Alison thought she was probably right.

Archie arrived back mid-morning with Joan and her daughter. From her balcony Alison could hear a much excited Margaret thank Archie for all his help and promise to 'return the favour' as soon as possible which prompted from Lauren a caustic, 'and we all know what she means by that mum don't we?' On any other day Alison would have called out to him but this morning she hung back and watched at a distance which was where she wanted to stay for the moment. She wondered what she was hoping to see, Margaret and Archie steal a kiss maybe, a hug or something she could identify as some form of attachment which would make her own assignation last night more acceptable to her. Why had she been so keen for Archie to stay away last night, so amenable to it? Was Lauren right, had she really been so calculating? One thing she was sure of, she couldn't stay in her room all day so she bravely packed her bag for the beach and tried to persuade Lauren to come with her.

'What's all this then mum, you hoping to get yourself under a sunshade before Archie emerges from his room?' Alison was beginning to believe in thought transference.

'No' she lied 'we don't want to stay in here all day, it's beautiful out there.' Her mobile phone was ringing and it was at the bottom of her bag, she stood looking at it.

'It'll be him you know' said Lauren with a small, choking laugh, 'well it'll be one of them won't it.' Alison threw her daughter a fierce glance and dug the phone out but missed the call. It had been Robert.

Panic set in.

'Oh no Lauren you didn't phone dad last night after you came in here, after you saw me and John? You didn't did you, tell me you didn't?'

'Actually no I didn't. I went back to the bar and sat up half the night talking to Romeo then came back here and waited outside until I saw lover-boy leave. I wonder what dad wants?'

'I have no idea and I'm probably not going to ring him back. Not at the moment anyway, I've got enough on my plate thank you. Now are you coming to the beach or not?'

Alison had found herself a quiet corner next to the beach surrounded by low growing shrubs spilling yellow trumpet-like flowers across the lawns. She was very comfortable on her sunbed and she had asked the gardener to lower the shade so that it eclipsed the top half of her body, now she felt truly hidden. Her book was open and she was turning the pages but none of it was going in, all she could think about was last night and she found herself wanting John, yet she was torn between excitement and guilt. She replayed his last words as he left her room last night, that they should tell everyone today. That they should come clean and not deny it any longer. Deny what she thought, what did she really feel for him after all this time, was it still love? The thought of confronting Archie with such news terrified her and no matter what John had said about his marriage she felt Milva would be devastated. This all left Alison in no doubt she must persuade John to do nothing, for now. She had to make him understand they were in the middle of an affair that had lasted thirty-five years but to their partners, or at least to Archie, this would be new and painful territory. Then she thought back to Archie's overnight stay with Margaret and Joan and wondered if she was secretly hoping that some spark had been lit between them so that she might gently let him down and Margaret could step in and make all well again. She shuddered at her cunning thoughts.

'You look like you're shivering, you can't be cold.' John was standing next to her with the sun behind him and she was glad to see his face. She pulled her knees up under her chin, an unnecessarily modest move and put her book to one side. 'Don't tell me you're reading, I haven't been able to concentrate all morning.'

She knew the feeling and was enjoying it. 'Did Milva notice you were late?'

'No. She'd had far too much to drink to notice anything. Told you she wouldn't miss me and it wouldn't have mattered if she had. Anyway she was fast asleep when I got back.' He picked up the book, 'I wish I'd brought a good book with me, it might have helped me get to sleep last night.'

'I expect Ali's got one you could borrow, she's got a suitcase full haven't you girl?' Archie was pulling a sun bed into the shade.

'You're back' she hoped she sounded pleased to see him but not as much as she hoped he hadn't heard any of their conversation.

'Lauren told me where to find you.' Alison made a mental note to thank her daughter when she saw her next. 'Got back about an hour ago.'

'Good trip?' asked John not moving from his seat on the edge of the sun bed as he sat there thumbing through the paperback and looking quite relaxed.

'Jack, it was magnificent. Being able to stay in one of those chattel houses is a fantastic experience, nobody should miss out on that. Why don't you take Milva over there, I bet she'd love it.' He turned to Alison, 'I've got so much to tell you, I don't know where to start' he laughed. 'We had a lovely drive back this morning, and watched all the locals going off to church, everyone goes to church here on a Sunday. Do you know Jack there are seventy-two churches on this island and there's only about ten thousand people live here.' Alison smiled at his attention to detail and wondered why that hadn't transferred to his appearance. He was lying back on the sun bed with his hands folded across his rounded body, wearing a selection of colours that might have been more at home on a television test card. His knees were showing signs of misplaced sun cream and his nose could have given Rudolph a run for his money. Then she looked at John, still sitting on the edge of her bed in khaki shorts and a white polo shirt, bronzed and slim, his grey hair falling across his face and she hated how he made her feel.

'Perhaps we should go' she could sense John smirking.

'Why not' said Archie 'we could all go and wash our sins away.' He was gesticulating and laughing heartily now and Alison wanted him to stop. 'It was a real sight Ali I wish I'd been able to share it with you.' She pushed her sunglasses into her face and complained of sun lotion in her eyes, then took a towel and wiped away the tears.

NINE

They had stayed in the shaded corner all afternoon, Alison and Archie, and when she went back to her room to change for dinner she was completely exhausted from having to deal with his exuberance whilst continuing to pretend everything was as it should be.

'So, what do you think' said Lauren 'do you suppose they got it together?'

'Archie and Margaret? No I don't think so.'

'Would be quite convenient for you if they did though wouldn't it?'

'Why do young people always seem to think sex is the answer?'

'And like you don't?'

Archie had phoned to say he would meet them in the bar as he needed to pop round to Margaret's room to help her with Joan who hadn't yet recovered from her fall, so Alison and Lauren walked up to dinner together through the gardens as the wind was beginning to lash through the palms.

'Maxwell said last night he'd heard there was a storm coming' said Lauren.

'Maxwell's Romeo's dad?'

'Yes. I was chatting to him last night too. He's a really nice man.'

'Runs in the family then?' Alison was sensing her daughters growing attachment to the handsome barman. 'Is Romeo working this evening?'

'He works most nights. I think he just turns up when his dad tells him to, he says he's lucky to have the job. It seems that most of the locals try to work in the tourist industry, some even at two or three different hotels.'

'Good job we're here then, keeping the economy healthy.' Alison could sense there was something else her daughter wanted to say. 'They sound very close, Romeo and his dad.'

'Romeo told me his dad's father died in a ferry accident that happened years ago.'

'Archie saw something about that in the Museum the other day, it was in 1970 I think and one of the ferries travelling from St Kitts capsized and most people on board perished.'

'It wasn't bad weather or anything, they had like twice as many passengers as they should have been carrying and it went down. Apparently Maxwell was on the beach watching the ferry come over from St Kitts and saw it all happen. That must have been horrible, watching it go down and knowing your dad was on board.' Alison thought her daughter was about to cry. 'Romeo said most families on the island were affected by the disaster and everyone helped each other.'

'That doesn't surprise me, they are genuine people here but it must have been awful for Maxwell who can only have been a young boy at the time. Funny isn't it how people are forced to cope with such tragedy in their lives and yet when you meet them you would never know. I suppose it's good to realise bad things won't always be the ruination of the human race.'

'I didn't ever think I'd get over you and dad splitting up and still now sometimes I find it really difficult to deal with, but to be honest after hearing about Maxwell I felt a bit guilty, I mean at least dad's still around. I expect Maxwell would love to pick up the phone and ring his dad.'

'You're doing really well, we're both very proud of you.'

'Hey what did dad want, did you ring him back?'

'Damn, no I forgot, too late now though. I'll call him in the morning. Now let's go and see if we can find Romeo and get him to make us a couple of rum punches.'

Archie wasn't in the bar but Milva and John were already there and deep in conversation with Romeo. Milva called them over when they came in and Alison fought hard to drag her eyes away from John as he leaned into the bar looking even better than he had done the night before.

'You missed a great debate last night Ali' said Milva putting her arm around Lauren, 'you've an 'A' student here, she's a bright kid. I enjoyed our discussion, I hope she didn't wake you up when she got back?'

'I didn't hear her come in.' Lauren narrowed her eyes as she looked at her mother and Alison felt suitably chastised. She glanced over at John who was swirling his whisky sour and wearing a half smile that was supposed to include only Alison in its significance but he was completely unaware that Lauren had walked in on them last night and now she too was party to their secret.

When Joan walked into the bar she was flanked by Archie and Margaret as they made slow progress towards the group. Archie was already making contact by shouting greetings across the room and trying to begin a conversation with Alison which she declined by pretending not to hear. Lauren had almost disappeared under her seat with embarrassment as they lumbered along to Archie's instructions of 'right a bit, left' and 'right hand down a bit' in an attempt to elevate the mood of the troupe. However Milva had seen the opportunity for fun and got up to move chairs and wave Joan into what she called her 'parking space'.

'God why does Archie have to be so embarrassing?' said Lauren under her breath.

'Well honey' said Milva 'we used to have a saying in the business "if you can't fix it, feature it", you should try it some time, it works.'

Milva insisted they all share a table at dinner and John and Archie took Joan steadily into the restaurant and Alison noticed Lauren hanging back and chatting with Margaret.

'She says Archie's been a real life saver this holiday' said Lauren quietly to her mother as they sat down to dinner, 'she says she doesn't know what she would have done without him at the weekend. She said he's really wonderful with "mummy". See I told you she fancies him.'

'What are you saying?' said Alison.

'Well, fix those two up and you can elope with John-boy over there. That is what you want isn't it mum?' But Alison knew life wasn't meant to be that easy.

John had positioned himself next to her all evening and Alison found it difficult to concentrate on any conversations around the table except those between John and his wife. She didn't enjoy her heightened sensitivity to their familiarity and tried to ignore it.

When Archie offered to help Margaret get Joan back to their room John jumped in and suggested he walk Alison back as Milva and Lauren were continuing last night's debate in the bar but this time they were including some of the other American guests. Alison watched as her daughter launched into her arguments with confidence and felt pride at the way she was handling herself. John came up and took her arm telling his wife that he would be back to hear her conclusions.

'Everyone seemed to be getting along tonight' said Alison when they were out of earshot, 'especially you and Milva.'

'Jealous are we?'

'I'm not a young girl John, of course I'm not jealous, just making an observation that's all.' She was lying of course, her stomach had flipped when he sat next to her at dinner and she was enjoying the acrobatics, whilst trying to convince herself any attention he was giving to Milva seemed insincere. The wind had got up as they headed back to the room. There was a full moon and it lit up the stormy sky, Alison stopped for a moment and studied it. He came up behind her and slipped his hands round her waist.

'What are you thinking? Constable, Turner?'

'Constable definitely, there isn't anyone who can beat him on clouds.'

'Now let me see' he moved away from her, pushed his hands into his pockets and walked backwards looking at the sky. 'I don't know about that, I think Friedrich could give him a run for his money you know.'

'I don't believe this' the voice came from behind them, it was Milva, 'what are you guys saying? Have you forgotten all about Thomas Cole?' Alison turned quickly to see John walking over towards his wife. 'There are plenty of great American painters around you know, you Europeans can't have it all your own way.' She was laughing now and Alison felt sure she must have arrived too late to see John holding her close just moments before.

'He was born in Lancashire' laughed John, 'you can't claim him as one of your countrymen.'

'Sure I can, he came over when he was just a boy and' she was enjoying the conversation and reinforcing her point with a finger, 'he didn't start painting until he was in the States, years after. So he's ours, not yours' she laughed, 'what do you think Ali, you're the art expert?'

'You're absolutely right, Cole saw himself as an American and he wouldn't want to be remembered any other way but I'm still thinking Constable.'

'Weymouth Bay?' John was standing between them both now like a referee before a fight and Alison wondered whose hand he would raise at the end of it all.

'He produced a Sketch for Weymouth Bay and that's what I'm seeing here' she said with enthusiasm looking up into the sky. Milva threw her head back and put her hands on her waist.

'Hell no, that's got Cole written all over it.' It was meant to end the conversation and of course it did.

Archie didn't get back until after midnight. Alison had sat on the balcony on her return and slowly drunk her way through their small drinks fridge. She watched him go into his room, then come out again onto his patio with a drink in his hand, like she had done. He sat there for some time and she watched him silently, in the dark, wondering if he too was facing conflict. Was Lauren right, had there been some connection between him and Margaret? He'd pushed off his shoes and fallen asleep and now the glass was hanging precariously in his hand. Then from out of the shadows Alison saw someone remove the glass and put it on the table, then kiss his cheek and walk away. It was Milva.

TEN

Alison had gone down early to breakfast on her own still confused by what she had seen last night. Milva's tenderness towards Archie had left many questions unanswered and she felt they would probably remain so as she was unable to broach the subject with him. She was sitting on the beach watching the pelicans dip and dive for food when her 'phone rang. It was Robert. Finding it difficult to break the habit of a lifetime, she started with an apology.

'Sorry I meant to call back earlier is everything alright?' After making her excuses she listened for over five minutes as her ex-husband talked. He began by asking how everyone was but not waiting for an answer and as the small talk continued Alison waited for the bombshell, she knew there had to be one, this was Robert.

'So you see I had to let you know, soon as. I just couldn't run the risk of Lauren phoning the twins and them blurting it all out. They're so excited you see. So you'll let her know then?' It was his turn to wait now. Eventually Alison answered.

'Do your dirty work for you, you mean?'

'Come on Alison don't be difficult.'

'Difficult?' she shrieked and one of the breakfasting pelicans pulled up on his dive and took off over the restaurant. 'Your timing has never been great Robert but you've excelled yourself this time. Why now, right in the middle of our holiday and just when she's starting to relax, why now?'

'Because contracts like this don't come along too often at my age and I can't let this one slide by, surely you can see that? And anyway it's not like I'm never going to see her again, it's only California.'

'Don't you see? She's only just got used to you living in north London for Christ's sake and for your information California is a long way from London, a bloody long way and she'll have the time difference to deal with. She won't be able to just pick up a 'phone and ring when she needs you.' She waited for a reply but got none. 'Have you really got to take it? There's no other way?' she was pleading with him now.

'I've already signed. It's done.'

'Well you wasted no time.'

'I have been calling you for over twenty-four hours.' She bit her lip, it was true she'd ignored his calls. 'Look you'll have to make her see it's not the end of the world and she can come over in the holidays. It'll be fun once she gets used to the idea.'

'I'll deal with it' she said and threw the mobile back into her bag.

With her appetite for breakfast lost Alison walked along the beach and made a plan for her conversation with her daughter. She would start by saying it was a fantastic opportunity for Robert to go and he had been very reluctant to take the job but hoped she'd go over to California during the holidays. Very quickly she threw out that plan and started again. She would say Robert had been forced into taking the job, no that was no good, next plan. He won't go if she didn't want him to, no good again and anyway not true because knowing Lauren she would probably say she wanted him to stay. She was still searching for a plan when John jogged down the beach towards her. He stopped and caught his breath.

'You're up early. I don't usually see anyone during my run. You okay?'

'Not really I've just had Lauren's dad on the 'phone with news that he's moving to California and would I just let her know.' She was furious and found it hard to disguise her anger. 'She's going to be devastated John, she still relies on her father such a lot and he just can't see it.'

'Well maybe you should work on getting another male role model into her life' he said pulling her towards him and trying to kiss her.

'I can't just move you in to replace him, he's her father' she said, transferring her anger to John now, 'this is really going to upset her and just at a time when she has so much else to deal with.' She started walking back towards the rooms and he walked quietly beside her, but listening now. 'She's got her exams coming up and then there's' she gave him a sideways glance, 'then there's you and me.'

'Look I've been thinking about that and I saw your face when I suggested we come right out and tell everyone we wanted to be together, you looked terrified at the prospect.'

'Well that and the fact it was three in the morning and my daughter was missing' they sat down on a low wall that skirted the gardens, close enough for them to see the rooms but far enough away for them both to sit and talk quietly. He was relaxed and in control again, his running vest was soaked through and clung to his body and she searched for any imperfections but found none.

'It's probably going to be better if we take this stage by stage. Go home and then let everyone know what's happening. I think you're right, if we do it here it will cause an unholy row and we don't want to cause any unnecessary pain do we?' *Unnecessary pain* thought Alison, such an interesting concept.

'Well it might be a bit late for that' she said bravely.

'What do you mean?'

'Lauren already knows John.' She heard his sharp in-take of breath.

'What do you mean "she already knows"? How does she already know?'

'I had to tell her, I had no choice.'

'I got to say I think you've made a big mistake there.' He was serious now, not flirtatious but for once he seemed to be grasping the severity of what was going on. 'How much did you tell her?'

'I told her everything' she sighed. 'I had to John she walked in on us the other night when you came back to my room.

'Jesus Christ Alison, you never told me that' he was almost

yelling.

'Well I'm telling you now aren't I.'

'Jesus Christ.'

'Well I know it's not ideal.'

'Ideal? You bet it's not ideal. What do you think she'll do, I mean can she be trusted?'

'I think perhaps she's more concerned about whether she can trust me. After all I did bring her on holiday with a man I'm already having a relationship with and then she walks in on me in bed with someone else. I don't see how you can ask such a thing of her actually.'

'I've upset you' he said taking her hands in his, 'and I'm sorry, I guess I just panicked. I'm sure she'll be fine.' Alison heard what he said but she wasn't sure she believed him.

When she got back to the room Lauren was awake and had ordered breakfast in the room.

'You can share mine if you like, I thought you'd have eaten by now' she said lifting her fork to her mouth as the coconut sauce dripped off the pumpkin pancake. 'Want some?' she offered.

'No I've not much of an appetite this morning. I've just spoken to dad.' She took up her position opposite her daughter knowing that she too was about to lose her appetite for breakfast. Alison told her as gently as she could without reference to any of the plans she had worked on whilst walking on the beach, there wasn't a simple way of telling her. After she'd finished Lauren sat staring at her breakfast and then she flung the fork back down onto her plate.

'So when do they go?'

'Within the month.'

'That's a real pisser mum.'

'I know sweetheart but he's very keen for you to go out there and visit.' Her daughter looked at her with empty eyes and she wished she hadn't said it, as if it was supposed to make everything better.

'Some people just don't deserve your love, do they mum?'

Alison had coerced Lauren into visiting Charlestown with her and Archie later that morning but managed to avoid telling her the purpose of the journey was to visit the Philatelic Bureau.

'Stamps? Archie collects stamps? Christ mum it gets worse with that bloke.' They were standing by the car waiting for Archie who had forgotten his suncream and judging by the back of his neck it wasn't the first time. Over by reception a taxi pulled up and Milva and John got in. As they passed Milva rolled down the window and leant out.

'We're going back to see the chattel houses this morning. Maybe see if we can fix up to stay overnight. Jack said Archie raved about them, he really made him want to go back and stay. So I guess we'll see you tomorrow when we get back?'

'That would be lovely' said Alison confused. Lauren was leaning over the car now and laughing with Milva.

'Have a great time and don't go trying the hammock.'

'You're too hard on Archie honey, he's a sweet guy' said Milva as they drove away.

'You didn't know they were going did you?' said Lauren.

'John might have mentioned it this morning when I saw him, I can't remember.' She was lying of course but consoled herself at how easy it was to forget to exchange information as she reflected on Milva's kiss last night. This feeling like a girl again had taken her by surprise but she embraced it without a care for who she might hurt. It might be that with John away from the hotel she could take a more balanced look at how she was feeling because right now every time she saw his face her stomach flipped. The girl inside was fighting against the mature woman who had long since left behind such frivolity. She had bowled headlong into her renewed affair unable to think about anyone who was important to her, she was so in love all else went out of the window. Perhaps if she was able to slow everything down she might be able to get a perspective on what was happening in her life and with John away until tomorrow evening she might have a chance to do that. She took a moment to remind herself that a few days earlier she had welcomed Archie's absence from the hotel for the very same reason.

Archie was calling out to them as he crossed the car park.

'Archie's back' and indeed he was, smeared in sun cream he had completely failed to rub into his face and neck. 'That didn't take long did it?' he smiled.

Charlestown was full of energy and delighted Lauren who leapt out of the car to buy one of everything from the fruit seller on the corner of the street. Alison felt it was quite unnecessary but her daughter saw it as a way to 'boost the economy' and 'get some money to go straight into the pockets of the locals.' Leaving Archie to park the car they found their way to the Philatelic Bureau or "Stamp Shop" as Lauren insisted on calling it.

'So what's John-boy doing taking Milva away for a night at the chattel houses?'

'They're on holiday they're bound to do things like that.'

'But I thought he couldn't bear to be away from you. What's he doing whisking his Mrs off for the night?'

'I really don't know Lauren, it's none of my business.'

'I just don't get it mum, they looked pretty together when they went off this morning. You sure he's for real? I mean it's not like he's got a great track record with you is it?' Her daughter's ability to get straight to point wounded Alison and yet she envied her directness.

Archie joined them and they went into the shop. It was a small wooden room with a glass-topped counter displaying hundreds of stamps. The assistant, whose badge told them she was Dolores, was patient and hugely helpful as Archie ploughed his way through all the stamps in the cabinet. He wanted to buy stamps that reflected the local architecture.

'I'm a builder by trade.'

'You are? Well that's a wonderful thing to be. To create good places for people to live out their lives is a virtuous thing to do.' She picked up one of the stamps on show and pushed it towards him. ''Now here is someone who some say was not so virtuous.' Archie picked up the stamp carefully.

'But that's Horatio Nelson, I thought you loved him over here?'

'Many loved him' said Dolores taking another stamp and pushing it towards Archie, 'especially this woman, Fanny Nisbet.' Archie inspected the stamp carefully.

'She's a good looking woman' he said.

'Yes and was very well connected on Nevis, some say that's why Nelson wanted to marry her but then he turned his eye to another.'

'Emma, Lady Hamilton' said Lauren unwilling to add any more than the basic facts.

'That's right and he broke the heart of the girl from Nevis.'

'That's sad' said Alison 'of course he's known as a great leader at home, children learn about him at school.'

'Ummm' said Dolores, 'and it just goes to show men who are driven by the appetite for greatness are not always so honourable.'

'And there ends the lesson for today' whispered Lauren in her mother's ear.

Archie had bought all the stamps he could find depicting the local buildings and Dolores fitted them into small individual envelopes and then packed them all into a larger envelope which for some reason, and no-one knew why, had a picture of Mickey Mouse on the front.

After lunch Lauren returned to her books and Alison went back to the room for a rest leaving Archie to his new collection of stamps. Alison could hear him from her balcony sharing his new find with anyone who would listen as they passed by and she realised the reason she had returned to her room was to avoid being on her own with him. She could hear her mobile ringing in the bedroom and when she got there to answer it Lauren had ended the call.

'Who was that?'

'Dad.'

'Why did you do that, he was probably ringing up to see how you've taken his news.'

'Exactly' said Lauren.

'Anyway you shouldn't have cut him off, he'll think it was me.'

'Mum why are you still so bothered about what he thinks of you? He hurt you really bad and yet still you're trying to be the good little wife.' She picked up her books and said, without looking her mother, 'you should be thinking of yourself a bit more now.'

Lauren had gone down to dinner early to chat with Romeo and Alison decided she would use the evening to focus on her relationship with Archie which, without John being around to distract her, would be easier she thought. There was no doubt Archie had saved her life after the divorce. He had employed her even though she hadn't worked for years and he had helped her get back her feeling of self-worth and start living again, she had a lot of reasons to be grateful to him. Her thoughts were drifting and she quickly pulled herself back into the here and now and tried to face her doubts but even as she sat thinking about her relationship with Archie she wanted John. When she thought about sex with Archie, she wanted John, when she thought about Archie making her laugh, she wanted John. How was she going to free herself from the conflict? There was only one way.

Lauren burst through the door, looking out of breath.

'Forgotten something?' asked Alison.

'You're not going to believe what I've just seen.' Alison waited.

'Only Archie and Margaret at it in his room.'

ELEVEN

' "At it"? '

'On the bed, him with his arms around her. Mum it was gross.'

'You could hear them?'

'The patio doors were open, they were facing the door mum, there's no mistaking what they were doing.'

'I can't believe that, of either of them, and anyway you can't possibly have known what was going on.'

'Look.' Lauren sat down in front of her mother. 'As I walked past his room I heard a woman laughing and when I looked in' Alison started to shake her head, 'mum it's dark outside and his lights were on, they were lit up like a fucking Christmas tree. Anyway she was saying something about never being able to forget what he'd done for her and then she started snogging his face off.'

'What was Archie saying during all this?'

'Don't know, he hadn't come up for air by the time I left. Mum aren't you getting this?' Alison looked confused. 'You come on holiday with the most boring bloke on the planet, during which holiday you meet the love of your life and tear yourself apart wondering how to let Archie down. This is it mum, this is your golden opportunity to dump the bloke because he's shagging around, of course you don't have to tell him you've be doing a bit of shagging around yourself this holiday but it's given you a way out mum, you must see that.' Lauren waited for her mother to say something but she just got her things together and went to leave the room. 'If you're quick you'll probably catch them at it.'

Alison waited at the bottom of the stairs, in the same place she had waited for John just a few days before, when he had taken her in his arms and she realised she was still in love with him. She heard Archie's patio doors bang shut and watched as Margaret ran across the garden back towards her own room. She went up to Archie's door and knocked as she went in. He called out from the bathroom.

'I'm in the shower, running a bit late I'm afraid. Tell you what, you and Lauren go ahead and I'll catch you up. Tell Romeo I'll have one of his special rum punches' he said laughing, 'I'm in the mood for a party tonight Ali.'

In the bar Joan waved them over.

'Come and sit with me. Margaret's not here yet, I don't want to sit on my own.'

'Where's Margaret?' asked Lauren mischievously.

'She said she wanted to have a walk in the gardens before it got dark and got a porter to drive me up here. I still can't walk properly you know.' She looked around. 'I see Archie's not here yet either, funny that.' Alison saw her thin lips break into a smile and thought that while, generally, smiling improved a person's appearance and made them more appealing, in the case of Joan the opposite was true. She placed a small bony hand, riddled with arthritis on Alison's knee, 'I think I did warn you, didn't I dear?'

'Lauren why don't you order the drinks' Alison said determined to change the subject, 'Archie said he'd like a rum punch' and she moved away from the old lady letting her hand fall onto the chair.

Archie and Margaret turned up together deep in conversation and Alison wondered whether they had planned to meet on their way to the bar or it had just been coincidence. She noticed a change in Margaret, she was beginning to brown and lose the awful pallor she had when they first arrived and she'd pulled her hair back from her face and tied it on top of her head, very much like Alison often did. Now it was possible to see Margaret was quite some years younger than she had first thought, maybe she was early or mid-forties and her initial disinterest in her appearance had been addressed tonight. Gone were the pale blue and beige outfits and in their place a full length, v-necked, chiffon dress in pink and white and a pair of sling-back wedges with a stacked heel that brought her almost to Archie's height. It was maddening how difficult it was to tell a person's age these days Alison decided, as she noticed some carefully applied pale pink lipstick and for some unexplained reason felt a sigh of relief when she saw it was still intact.

'She's made a big effort tonight' whispered Lauren to her mother as she came back to the table. 'You must see it now mum, it's obvious, just look at the pair of them.' Alison did look and she saw Margaret had slipped her arm into Archie's and was intent on their conversation. Lauren had looked across and saw Joan was watching Alison's reaction, she nudged her mother and nodded towards the old lady who was starting to say something. Alison leaned forward to hear and she spoke quietly into her ear.

'They make a lovely couple don't you think?' she was laughing but got no reaction from Alison. Her face straightened and she leaned in again, 'you'd be a fool to ignore it you know, my daughter just can't help herself.' Alison pulled herself back into her seat.

'How can you talk about your own flesh and blood like that, she's your daughter.'

'Leave it mum, she's not worth the effort. Let's go into dinner, Maxwell's put us at a rail table and he says there's a fantastic view of the stars tonight.' She tugged at her mother's arm, 'come on mum, leave the old witch. Let's eat.'

Starry nights have always left Alison speechless so her quiet demeanour throughout dinner was easily excusable. Archie was charming company and Lauren seemed to be trying extra hard to get along with him and when he left the table for the restroom she turned to her mother and asked her if she was alright. Alison was glad she had asked but was unable to give her an answer.

'I think it's decision time mum, you've got to front it with Archie about Margaret, you can't just let it slide. I mean even if you don't intend to spend the rest of your life with the bloke you can't let him piss you about like this.'

'And what about the way in which I've *pissed him* about Lauren? Does my behaviour excuse his in any way? Should I find what he has done, or should I say might have done, any more acceptable because of what happened between me and John the other night? Really, do I have any right to question what happened earlier considering that I'm thinking about ending it with him anyway?' Lauren looked at her in astonishment.

'Christ mum I didn't ask for your life story, it's a simple question, who do you want to be with, John or Archie?' Alison didn't answer her daughter. 'Oh my God you still don't know do you?'

It was Tuesday and they had been on the island a week and Alison felt she was quite acclimatised now. Her body clock had adjusted and she absolutely refused to take a cardigan with her when she went out in the evening. The first few days of the holiday, that Archie had referred to as their 'settling-in period', had been a roller coaster for Alison but she now felt strong enough to make some important decisions. Today was the day she was going to sort out the rest of her life. John and Milva had returned to the hotel and were sitting on the beach not far from where Alison had pulled a sun bed into the shade. She watched like a spy as they took out their books, crossed one leg over the other, pushed on their sunglasses and began to read in unison. Everything they did seemed to have a rhythm to it, they were in sync and she sensed a harmony to their movements or was it just because they had been together for so long they mirrored each other's actions as married people sometimes do after many years of being together. Although if she was honest with herself she and Robert hadn't ever achieved such a rapport, more than that her ex-husband had actively worked against any synergy between them, preferring they should remain 'free spirits'. 'And look where that got us' said Alison out loud taking her mobile out of her bag and seeing Robert had made yet another call to add to the others she had declined to take.

'You talking to yourself Ali?' Archie pulled up another sun bed alongside.

'Only muttering' she put her mobile away. 'I'm afraid Robert has been making waves again.'

'No change there then but we don't want anything to spoil the holiday do we, not now Lauren seems to be having such a good time?' He began plastering sun crème on his body and Alison noticed even Archie had begun to take on a Caribbean glow. His red knees were brown now and looked good next to his saffron coloured shorts. There was definitely something about Archie that was different and Alison wondered if there was a magic about Margaret that had something to do with his transformation but still couldn't decide whether that was something that disturbed her or not. 'So what's he done this time?'

Alison went through the order of yesterday's events that had been so carefully avoided at dinner last night. Archie continued to apply his sun crème as she talked which was a practical distraction she found useful as it allowed her to relieve herself of her deep regret at Robert's move to the States. It was strange how doing the ordinary things during a time of trauma gave a balance to dealing with the problem. After she had finished Archie lay back on his sun bed and placed his wide brimmed hat over his face.

'Is that it Archie? You've nothing to say?'

'Nothing to say that would make any difference, no' he replied.

'Thanks. Pointless asking me what the problem was then.'

'I don't think so. You've got it off your chest now, so maybe we can get on and enjoy the rest of our holiday.'

'I wish it was that easy.'

'Now I don't know a lot about families Ali but when I was building houses I used to find there were two kinds of problems. One kind of problem you could go around and try and keep everybody happy and the other you had to go right through and not be afraid of stepping on a few toes but either way you had to let people have their say and once they'd done that everyone felt ready to get things done.'

'And which kind of problem is this then? The kind you go around or the kind you go right through?'

'I don't have to tell you that Ali, you already know you're never going to keep everybody happy.'

At six o'clock Lauren joined them on the beach to watch the sun go down. Romeo brought over some drinks and as the sun slipped below the horizon Alison felt all the stress of the day disappear with it. John and Milva had returned to their room much earlier for an afternoon nap and stopped off to arrange a meet for dinner later that evening. Milva had been full of enthusiasm for her night at the chattel houses and engaged Archie while Alison tried to read John's face and decide whether it had been a success for him too. His face told her nothing, yet there was a hint of sadness about him as if in fact his marriage to Milva was coming to an end as he had insisted and he had the gloom of inevitability about him, unlike his wife who was launching into yet another anecdote about the previous evening. Alison reminded herself of Milva's background, the woman was an actress and used to playing a part, so she wouldn't find it too difficult to adopt the role of happy holidaymaker in the face of the other guests. After all who would want to display any real heartache in front of those they barely knew and Alison shuddered when she thought that she herself didn't come into the category of those *barely known* but Milva would be unaware of that, or would she?

'Only three more sunsets to go' said Archie putting his arm around her. 'I think this holiday is turning out to be a bit of a hit with you-know-who' he said nodding towards Lauren who was walking back towards the bar with Romeo. 'Doubt whether she'll want to go home. How about you Ali, do you want to go home?'

'I love it here, but home is where I belong' was what Alison said out loud but inside her head a voice cried out, *home is where I get to start my new life with John.* And there it was brief and to the point Alison's sudden realization of where she wanted to be and just who she wanted to be with. Up until that point she had been quite undecided about whether she could throw herself back into a relationship with John, whether what she was feeling was real but in the face of Archie's honest question suddenly she knew. She now knew she wanted to be with John, she had arrived at the truth at last but the shame of it was the truth had arrived together with Archie's arm warmly wrapped around her shoulders but now feeling like a dead weight as she longed to shrug it off. They sat together looking out to sea as darkness fell around them and Alison struggled with the deceit of it all but knew that none of it was planned. How could she have known that here, on this tiny island, the man she had always loved best of all would re-enter her life just at the time she felt things were becoming less complicated with this simple, straightforward and honest man who was sharing her view of the ocean.

Back in the room Alison rejected yet another call from Robert.

'He hates not knowing what's going on doesn't he mum?' said Lauren half smiling. 'I'm almost enjoying keeping him in the dark.'

'He only wants to know how you've taken his news I expect. I should talk to him really but now is not the right time, I'll do it tomorrow. It's just I don't know what to say. I can't say you've taken it well can I because you haven't really but then I don't want to get into a pointless debate with him. I mean the decision's already been made, there's nothing to be done really.' She pulled out a white silk dress from the wardrobe. 'I'm dreading tonight. I'm finding these cosy little dinners very difficult now that I know how I feel about John.' It was said to prompt the question from her daughter.

'So you've made your mind up at last then?'

'I love him Lauren, I suppose I've always loved him. I think if it had finished at the time, if he had told me himself that it was over I might have been able to forget him but that never happened.'

'Ah yes, Michael the Messenger.'

'I know it must sound ridiculous but he's always been present in my mind and now that I find myself' she paused, 'well not exactly footloose and fancy free but unmarried and free to choose, I choose him, I choose John.'

'And what about you-know-who?' Lauren nodded towards Archie's room, 'not that I'm over bothered about him, I mean I never thought you were good together, he's a dick.'

'Lauren' snapped Alison.

'Well he is' Lauren was laughing, 'this John-bloke is much more your type.'

'I'll explain everything to Archie when we get home.'

'I thought you said John-boy was up for doing it right here and now?'

'He was but I think he's changed his mind about that now. I had to tell him you knew everything and that you walked in on us the other night.' Lauren rolled off her bed laughing.

'Oh my god I wish I'd been there. You can tell he really fancies himself.'

'Do you think so?'

'You're joking aren't you? Course he does, he's your original Mirror-Man. You'll need one in every room mum if you set up house with him' and she disappeared into the bathroom.

The white silk dress was cool and the full skirt billowed in the breeze as Alison knocked on Archie's room door. Her hair was piled up on top of her head and fixed in place with a turquoise clip. He opened the door and gave a short gasp.

'You look a real picture tonight Ali' he said taking her arm. 'I want to take the long way round so I can show you off.' She couldn't respond to Archie's loving words. 'You're speechless' he was laughing, 'I've embarrassed you, again? Archie's always doing that I think.'

'Of course you haven't embarrassed me, it's nice to see you notice how I look' she lied and then tried to over-compensate which is always a big mistake, 'and you look good too this evening.' He stood back from her so she could take in his whole ensemble: the over-long white trousers that were, after a week, suffering from the nightly walk to the bar through the gardens, the half laced shoes which always made Alison wonder why Archie didn't buy slip-ons and the collared shirt with an hibiscus design in blue and pink. Archie tugged at the sleeve.

'Bought this off one of the beach vendors. It was a toss-up between this and electric green pineapples' he said and Alison was suddenly grateful for small mercies. 'I think I made the right decision' he said thoughtfully. 'Truth is I wanted to buy them both.'

'I didn't realise you had such a passion for clothes you always seem to dress so conservatively at home.'

'I suppose it's a new me. I felt like it was time, after years of being influenced by my dear old mum, for me to experiment with my own likes and dislikes. She was a big fan of brown and blue and I suppose I didn't have anyone else I was dressing for at the time. Anyway with the company to run and an invalid mother to look after I didn't get much time for dressing up. Then after she died I wanted to throw out my entire wardrobe but I was too mean so I invested in a couple of Argyle jumpers instead and discovered an interest in golf.' He smiled at her and pulled her in close, 'you don't suppose I've left it too late do you?' She said nothing but thought he probably had.

John took the seat next to hers at dinner and at every opportunity he allowed them to touch: a movement of his chair, his napkin, his glass and she welcomed him each time. The table had looked beautiful when they sat down and even the addition of elbows and arms couldn't detract from the delight it gave Alison. It was a dark night with cloud covering the moon and stars making the small white lights strewn around the rail all the more vivid. There was a slight breeze that every so often rearranged the clouds and allowed a star or two to appear then disappear again rapidly. As usual the restaurant was brilliantly lit by an array of candles so when the rail lights flashed a couple of times then completely disappeared in amongst the shrubbery it wasn't immediately obvious there had been a power cut.

TWELVE

Maxwell assured them the generator would swing into action within minutes and they should keep their seats. As they waited Milva made comparisons with the New York power outage in '77 and tried to draw Alison into the conversation. Alison however was trying to deal with Milva's husband whose hand was rising and falling along her thigh and making it difficult for her to concentrate and her lack of attention seemed to fire Milva into action.

'So what do you think Jack? Does this put you in mind of '77? Remind me what it was you were supposed to be doing that night? Sorry did I say *supposed*?' She drank from her glass which Maxwell repeatedly filled as an apology for the power cut. Alison felt Jack's hand freeze on her leg and very quickly he removed it as he got up to leave the table.

'I'm going to go see what the problem is.'

'I'm sorry sir but if you could remain seated' Maxwell was at his shoulder with another bottle of wine, 'it won't take long now but it's much safer if you stay where you are until we can bring in the lamps to light the floor and we can get you safely back to your rooms.' John sat down, leaned into his chair and sighed.

'I forget where I was' he said to his wife.

'I don't think you do honey, I think you know darn well where you were.' She was almost yelling now and the table fell silent. She took another drink and began to laugh, 'oh I can remember now, you were at the game weren't you sweetie?'

'If you say so.'

'It was you who said so' she snapped. Maxwell was waiting to fill her glass and she looked up at him. 'Are you always where you are supposed to be Maxwell?' she asked him.

'I try to be ma'am.' It was the perfect answer and the table fell silent again.

'So tell me Maxwell, do you get a lot of these power cuts here?' Archie sounded as if he actually wanted to know and wasn't simply trying to move the conversation on.

'Well sir, I hear you talking about the 1970's and I can tell you the electricity went off at four o'clock every afternoon during the 70's.' He gave a low melodic hum 'yes sir, every afternoon but things are much better now and I don't know if we have a problem with the generator or there's some weather giving a problem here but we'll soon have things fixed up. Now sir can I get you anything else?' Archie didn't have time to answer.

'Archie there you are,' Margaret descended on the table, 'mummy wants to go back to the room and they don't have anyone who can take us just yet and you know mummy, she wants to go right now, so they've found us a golf buggy. I hate to ask but could you help?' She turned to the rest of the table as though they were a second thought, 'promise I won't keep him long.'

Up until now Lauren had been quietly sipping her rum punch and enjoying Milva's cabaret but now she was ready to transfer her attention to the surprise guest.

'Go on Archie, you know you love to help out a damsel in distress' she said sucking on her straw. Alison tried a hard stare but thought Lauren probably couldn't quite see her.

Without any further persuasion Archie got up to leave the table.

'Archie don't mind helping out.'

'Oh you're a proper life saver, I'll just tell mummy' and Margaret kissed him gently on the cheek prompting another contribution from Lauren.

'I think you're in there Arch.'

'Jack'll see you all back to the room I expect' he said with an innocence that pained Alison as Lauren stretched under the table and gave her leg a nudge and leaned in towards her mother.

'It's all going on right under your nose mum.'

Alison knew every time she ignored Margaret's flirting with Archie, every time she offered his services to help with Joan, she knew she was encouraging the relationship. To her it was simple, any interest Archie or Margaret might have in one another would be a good thing because it could deflect his attention away from her. She was becoming a game player and she hated it. Maxwell appeared with a lamp and Alison quietly watched Archie's back as he took Margaret's arm and walked towards the waiting buggy. Milva was tutting loudly and shaking her head.

'Why do you tease the poor man so, Lauren? Don't you know a good man when you see one?' and Alison didn't know why, perhaps it was in defence of her daughter or because of the midnight kiss she witnessed on Archie's patio or maybe even being under cover of darkness that gave her the courage but she turned to Milva and asked.

'And you Milva, do you know a good man when you see one?' The table fell silent apart from a very quiet *'mum'* from Lauren that came out in two syllables. There were strings of sentences in Alison's head that she might have used in response to Lauren's obvious reprimand but she chose none of them and decided to remain mute, she thought it was the best decision. Afterwards she wasn't sure.

'You're asking me?' said Milva tilting her head to one side, 'Me? Well I don't know Jack-shit.' She was almost yelling as she scraped her chair back across the floor and Maxwell appeared asking her to stay at the table until he brought another light. 'Forget the light Maxwell, I'm a big girl now, I'll be just fine.' She disappeared into the darkness with Maxwell in her wake and at the same time John got up from the table and turned to Alison.

'Why did you have to say that? Just look what you've gone and done now.'

'It was hardly mum's fault she obviously touched a raw nerve.'

'Yes well the less said about your contribution the better.' He turned his back on them and went off in the direction of his wife. Alison was speechless. She turned to Lauren, with just the two of them left at the table now she suddenly had an urge to cry. It was a stupid urge and she fought it but without success and Lauren put her arms around her mother and rocked her gently.

'Some fucking holiday this has turned out to be.'

There is something about a table that's been deserted by its diners. The last time Alison had seen this was in New York in '77 when, just like tonight, the lights had gone out and people had left hurriedly. There were no napkins carefully folded, no glasses drained, no plates cleared. It was as though everyone had evaporated and left behind were the remnants of their evening at the once beautiful table. The single candle in the middle of the table burned still and Alison stared into it and tried to control her breathing as she felt panic rise in her.

'I've got to go and see if I can find Milva, I can't leave things like this.'

'Are you sure that's a good idea mum, aren't you better letting John deal with it?'

'I can't Lauren, she knows, well she knows something, I'm just not sure exactly what but what I don't want is her revealing everything to Archie.'

'But wouldn't that make your job easier, I mean he's got to know sometime if you're going to wander off into the sunset with John-boy.'

'Don't be silly, that isn't what she's going to be telling him though is it? She'll tell him John and I had an affair over thirty years ago and Archie will say, "well that's okay, that was then and this is now". He'll think it's a thing of the past and then I come along and tell him that we've decided to wind the clock by thirty-odd years and are giving it another go. It will crucify him Lauren.'

'You're right mum that stinks.'

As Alison left the restaurant and turned towards her room she saw only the odd lamp dotted around the grounds. Outside some of the guests were sitting and drinking in candlelight, she could hear them talking and laughing and wondered where Archie was right now. Was he talking and laughing with Margaret or were they rolling around on the bed together as Lauren had suggested earlier? Lauren wouldn't lie about that sort of thing so there must have been something in it but then maybe Margaret had fallen on top of him by accident and then without a moment's hesitation Alison found herself inside a *Carry On* film with Sid James and Barbara Windsor. She forced herself back into the moment and away from the terrifying Windsor cleavage. Towards the beach the staff had erected two lines of flares that glowed orange in the dark night and she was drawn towards them, not because that was the direction she wanted to go in but because their warmth and energy attracted her as an alternative to the dark walk back to the room. She would have her conversation with Milva but first she would collect her thoughts, just as she had tried after Robert had 'phoned and she knew she needed to talk to Lauren. She had been unsuccessful then as well.

When she reached the beach she sat on one of the small wooden tables where she and Archie often had lunch and she would watch him wrestle with his lobster or suck the meat from a crab claw. The ocean was noisy and she could feel the breeze and decided this was probably the coolest she had felt all holiday, right here on this seat.

'You need a wrap on evenings like these' Milva sat down beside her. 'Jack always laughs when I try and push one in my bag but hey I could sure use it now.'

She had been crying, it was easy for Alison to tell and she wondered if she might know the same of her. Alison jumped straight in.

'I'm sorry I upset you at dinner.'

'You didn't upset me.' She stressed the *upset* word and Alison wasn't sure if she was playing with her choice of English or if she meant it was more than that, more than upset. 'I usually love the breeze you get on this beach, not tonight though.' She looked around, 'I could do with a drink.'

'I think they've stopped serving down here now, because of the power cut.'

'Oh yeah, the power cut. Did it take you back to '77?'

'Did it take you back?' asked Alison and bit her lip. Too brave, she thought, too brave. She fumbled, 'what I meant was..'

'I know what you meant Ali.'

'Please don't say you know what I meant if you don't.

'I'm an American, I always say what I mean, we leave dancing around the facts to you Brits.'

'Is that what you think we do? Dance around the facts?'

'Sure you do. Think about it.'

'Perhaps we can be guilty of never saying what we mean.'

'What do you mean 'perhaps'? Look I've not been married to a Brit for all these years and learned nothing.' She paused and seemed to consider her next question. 'What do you think of Jack?' It was the question Alison was least prepared for.

'What do you mean think of him?'

'See there that's just what I was saying, I ask you a straight question and what d'you do but reply with another question. Now if that isn't dancing around the facts what is? So, tell me what do you think of my husband?'

'Alright, alright, I think he's charming. He's charming and good company and he's funny, well amusing, sort of.'

'What else?' It was said in a low voice, almost threatening.

'Well I don't know what else I mean he seems very nice, very straightforward. He's always seemed very plain speaking to me.' Alison wasn't just dancing she was positively doing a highland fling.

'How about trustworthy? Do you think he's trustworthy Ali?'

'I really don't know. Why are you asking me?' She was almost out of breath now and could feel her heart pounding in her chest.

'Why wouldn't I ask you? You're a Brit, maybe you understand where he's coming from. I used to think all British men were like Jack and then I got to know Archie and boy I found how different they all can be.'

'I wasn't aware you'd got to know Archie that well.'

'Good. I'm glad about that, I asked him not to tell you about our little chats.'

'Tell me what?'

'Oh Ali don't look so shocked all couples have secrets, you must know that.' Alison turned to go but Milva's voice softened. 'For Christ's sakes sit down Ali, don't you walk out on me too.'

'Who's walking out on you?'

'Jack, probably.'

'I'm so sorry.' It was the best she could do. 'You say "probably"?'

'It's the way he's being with me, you know, he's here but he's not really here. Hell Ali you know, a woman can sense when something's not right.' Alison gave an involuntary laugh.

'Don't ask me about that my ex-husband's mistress was five months pregnant before I even knew she existed.' She was laughing about it, this was the first time since Robert had come home from the office, poured her a drink and said "he had something to tell her" that she had been able to distance herself from it sufficiently well to find it, almost hysterical. 'Ridiculous isn't it? You would have thought I might have had some idea what was going on but oh no not me. There must have been signals but I just didn't see them.'

'Or you ignored them?'

'Can't you do that? Ignore them?'

'I wish.' Alison wondered if it was time to leave but she was close now, as close to finding out just exactly what Milva did know about her affair with John. 'So Ali if you had found out about your ex's affair do you think you'd have thrown him out?'

'I can't say, I honestly can't. I think I could have forgiven him anything really and after all it was him who decided he was leaving, I never asked him to go.'

'What about if you'd discovered his affair but it was with someone you knew, someone you'd actually come to like. How would you feel then?'

'I'm not sure what you're getting at' lied Alison.

'Let me tell you something about my charming husband.' She took a breath. 'Just before we got married Jack had an affair.'

'And you forgave him?' Alison prepared herself but she wasn't quite sure what for.

'Honey I didn't even know.' Her words shook Alison and she fought to control her expression. This couldn't be right, Michael had told her Milva had found out about their affair and it had to stop. He said Milva knew. 'I only found out recently' she went on.

'How did you find out after all this time?' said Alison hoping John hadn't already had the promised conversation with his wife.

'I found out because the whole sordid thing has begun again. Can you believe it and after all these years?'

'So he's told you?' The only way was forward now and Alison held her breath waiting for the worst.

'Hell no, *he's* not told me. *She's* the one who told me.'

'She?' It was a small voice and Alison wasn't even sure Milva had heard, so she said again, 'she?'

'Before we were married Jack had an affair with his cousin's girlfriend. Do you remember the other evening we were talking about the power outage?'

'And he was at the game?'

'Well he was supposed to collect me from the theatre that night and he didn't?'

'Were you expecting him?'

'Sure I was but he didn't turn up.'

'But he probably set off to meet you and got caught up in the crowds.'

'When I saw him the next day his face was a mess, he could barely speak and he said he'd been mugged on his way to get me, but that was a lie.' Alison could barely hear the loud talking American now as her voice became no more than a whisper. 'A lie that's lasted our whole marriage.' Alison leaned in towards her and struggled to listen. 'I found out the truth just before the holiday.' She took a long breath. 'Before we got married Jack shared a flat with his cousin, Michael and the truth is when his cousin got home that night he found Jack and his girl making out in the bedroom. He blew a fuse and beat Jack up.' Milva stared down at the table. 'Michael, that's Jack's cousin, he was a fire fighter and Jack guessed the power outage would keep him out late that night so he and Geena could meet at the flat. They guessed wrong.'

'So this affair you say that's going on again now, it's with this woman, Geena?'

'Well Jesus I hope so, otherwise I might have more than one problem on my hands.' She was trying to laugh and Alison thought she might not be able to stay a moment longer. 'No you're right, it's Geena and we were so close, she and I, we've always been close, more so since Michael died.' The words stung Alison and she held her breath. 'Poor Michael he went down with the Twin Towers.' It was too much and Alison began to cry, uncontrollably. 'Hey look I didn't mean to shock you. I'm a New Yorker and we have to deal with it every day, so yeah sometimes it does sound like we're talking about a traffic incident but hell if we stopped to think about the enormity of it all we'd never get up in the morning would we, but it doesn't mean every one of us isn't aware of what happened there. We all feel the loss, every day, we just deal with it, that's all.'

'I'm sorry it was just such a shock' but she didn't say why.

'Sure it was. Anyway long story short' she was starting to sound a little tired, 'Geena and I got real close since the tragedy. Got on so well, just like sisters and about a year back she started dating this guy, and getting her life back together again, doing normal stuff. Then a couple of weeks ago I was walking through Central Park and I see him, this guy, and I call out and he walks away from me. So I went round to his house,

I mean I was worried you know, he was acting weird. When I get there he says he and Geena aren't seeing each other any more and if I wanted to know why I should ask Jack.'

'So you did?'

'Nope. I asked Geena.'

'Why?'

'Because I was afraid he'd lie to me and I knew Geena couldn't.'

'That was very brave of you.'

'She told me everything well I don't think she left anything out 'cause it was about as bad as I could have expected it to be. About the affair they had before we got married, how Michael discovered it and stopped it going any further. She said Michael was distraught when he discovered them and she loved Michael I know she did. He blamed Jack for the whole thing and I can see why he might have done that. Anyway when she started dating again after Michael's death suddenly Jack was going round to her place and she said they couldn't help it, it just started again. She was crying, I was crying, Jesus it was the worst night.'

'Do you blame her?'

'I'm not sure, I know Jack can be real charming, you just said so yourself, and she said he told her he'd made the wrong decision all those years ago, that he should have chosen her and not me. She told me that, she actually told me that. But she wasn't mad when she was telling me it was almost like it was her excuse for it all happening. But what a thing to say, hey Ali, he made the wrong decision in choosing me.'

'What a truly terrible thing for him to say' whispered Alison, 'are you very angry with her?'

'Angry? Hell no, I feel sorry for her, I mean what kind of a dumb bitch would believe that kind of crap? I thought she was smart but hey not after that, except for one thing.'

'What was that?'

'Well she promised not to tell him about our conversation, not tell him that I'd found out about their affair, both their affairs actually. She said she wouldn't speak to him until after our holiday so as to give me time to decide what to do.'

'That's a bizarre display of sisterhood on any level.'

There followed silence and during the silence the power was restored. Not immediately but piece by piece across the hotel. It started with just a few lights in the restaurant, then the rooms started to come alive again and small footpath lights began to blink into life. Across the gardens small white lights intermingled with the trees, grew brighter and Alison looked up to see the rail in front of the restaurant glittering loudly and she wondered if it might be prophetic as she looked over at the American woman crumbled in the chair beside her and unable to contain her fury any longer she shouted out loud.

'What a fucking bastard he is.'

'Excuse mum's language Milva, she never swears', laughed Lauren appearing out of the shadows, 'someone must have made her really cross.'

THIRTEEN

It had been years since Alison had talked through the night and yet she wasn't sure why it had taken so long to explain her conversation with Milva to her daughter. On reflection it all seemed very straight forward, John had been dishonest with her.

'Not sure I can face the pancakes this morning, how about you?' Lauren looked up from the room service menu. 'You look exhausted mum.'

'You must think me a real fool.' Alison felt she might start to cry and got up to push open the windows onto the balcony. She curled up on the small sofa and pulled her legs up under her aware there had been no movement downstairs since John and Milva had returned to their room last night.

'It's not your fault he's turned out to be such a shit.' Alison put her finger to her lips and Lauren continued her assault on John in a loud whisper. 'Well at least you know where you stand with Milva now. She obviously hasn't a clue he had an affair with you too when they were engaged. What will you do now?'

'I'd like to know why it was that Michael 'phoned me all those years ago and said Milva had found out about our affair. If he was angry with John all he had to do was tell me what had been going on with him and Geena to truly foul things up between us.'

'Why? Why would that matter now? You're just looking for ways to try and forgive him. He's a shit mum, accept it.'

'I haven't stopped loving him because of what I heard last night.'

'Well you've got to front it with him then.'

'But if I do I'll break Milva's confidence and I don't think I can do that to the poor woman, she's suffered enough.'

'Mum she's still suffering. Why doesn't she just tell him she knows about the affair with Geena? Christ I would.'

'Finding out your husband had an affair while you were planning your wedding is one thing but finding out it's started again after thirty-odd years is a bit hard to swallow, especially the bit about him saying he "chose the wrong girl" all those years ago.'

'That was part of his pillow talk the other night wasn't it?'

'It certainly was.'

'Perhaps he's senile and just repeating himself.'

'Is my life really so ridiculous to you?'

'Not ridiculous no, I just don't get why you've still got so much time for him after what Milva told you last night. I can't believe you even want to see him again. Mum he's having an affair right now, back in the States, with the woman he was screwing while he was screwing you thirty years ago and mum and' she leaned over and pulled her mother towards her, 'he's telling you both the same thing. I mean how fucking sad is that?'

Alison was surprised she slept after breakfast and decided it was probably her daughter's summing-up technique that had given her some clarity. When she awoke Lauren had left a note saying she had gone down to the beach. She looked at her mobile, it was three in the afternoon and she'd slept through two missed calls from Robert.

She was standing in the shower when her mobile rang again. She let it ring when she saw it was John. Pulling the towel around her she looked in the mirror, no lies here. It seemed everything was written on her face and she wondered how she would leave the room and face everyone. Not just John but Milva and Archie too. The bedroom door banged and Lauren called out.

'Mum you have got to get yourself down to the beach Archie's being a real pain.' Alison came out of the bathroom and found her daughter sprawled on the bed. 'He never stops talking about you and what's worse is he asked Milva and John-boy to join us on the beach. So there we all were, in a row, facing the sea and it was surreal mum. Anyway I decided to come back to do some work and John walked back with me.'

'Did he ask about me?'

'He asked where you were and I said you were sleeping.'

'Nothing else?'

'Oh yeah and he asked if you were free for a shag this evening. For Christ's sake mum of course nothing else, I'd have told you wouldn't I? Anyway, I told Archie I'd send you down to the beach. You've got to go mum and put him out of his misery.' Alison's mobile began ringing again. 'That your 'phone?'

'It'll be John. He's called four times in the last ten minutes. I don't know what to say to him.'

'You should tell him to get lost.'

'Lauren, that's not very helpful you know.'

'Just feeling protective towards my mother.' There was a tap on the door. 'Christ do you think that's him? Shall I get it?'

'No you stay where you are I'll handle this.' Alison flung back the door and had to steady herself against the wall as Lauren shrieked and seemed to lift off the ground and propel herself through the doorway.

'Dad' and like a small child she flung her arms around his neck.

'I've been calling you for days' he was smiling at Alison. 'I was in the States sorting out..' he hesitated and looked at his daughter.

'She knows Robert I told her days ago.'

'Good, yes, so anyway I was there sorting out my move and thought, why not just drop in. They've got plenty of flights to St Kitts, easy.' Alison thought he looked a little nervous and decided he was probably right to.

'Drop in?'

'Yes, you know, see how my big girl is.' He drew Lauren towards him and Alison could see there was no-where else she would rather be. 'So how's it all going then? Good holiday?' Still nervous.

Alison was still and silent, just as she used to be when they were married and Robert had created yet another tricky situation. Lauren however had no such reservations.

'You wouldn't believe what's been going on here.' Alison shot her a glance and she did a double check. 'Yeah well it's been quiet mostly.' Robert waited. 'And I've met this bloke, Romeo, you'd like him and' she had run out of things she was able to talk about, things that weren't off-limits. 'Anyway we're going home in a couple of days. How long can you stay?'

Alison walked off onto the balcony as father and daughter exchanged information, allowable information that is and she began to feel it wasn't her right to limit the conversation. Although it was difficult to know what she could share with Robert, not that he'd care anyway but they led different lives now and it wouldn't have been right to allow him into the private side. Lauren had disappeared to the bar to bring back what she always referred to as the 'killer cocktails'.

'You came to check up on me, to see if I'd told her didn't you?'

'I came because you wouldn't answer your mobile and I wanted to know how she'd taken the news we were moving. What was I supposed to do, just guess she was alright? Why didn't you pick up when I rang?'

'I missed your calls.'

'All fourteen of them?'

'Crikey was it as many as that?' She liked the way he looked today, she didn't much like *him* these days but she always thought he was an interesting looking man. Being in the music business had given him an edge, put him a bit off-centre, a bit of a challenge she supposed and on reflection he was definitely that.

'How did she take it?'

'She was fine.' She almost choked on her choice of words, "fine". She hated words with so many meanings and fine came at the top of her list. 'Actually she wasn't, fine. She was seriously pissed off with you.'

'Not like you to sound so worked up.' He was leaning over the balcony looking far too relaxed and she had a sudden urge to grab his ankles and tip him over the rail.

'Perhaps it's the heat' she forced herself back into the bedroom to avoid a manslaughter charge just as Lauren reappeared with the drinks. 'Where are you staying?'

'Just across the way actually' and he nodded towards Archie's room. 'First floor and it was a coincidence I actually didn't know which room was yours.'

'So how did you find us then?' asked Lauren already half way through her rum punch.

'Some bloke downstairs told me where you were.'

'Perhaps it was Archie' said Lauren.

'No, he sounded American, bit of a pompous arse actually.'

'That'll be John then' snorted Lauren unable to control her giggling and blowing most of her rum punch down her nose. Robert got the signal and went on.

'Middle-aged men with long hair.' He tutted and shook his head.

'You've got long hair.'

'Ah yes but I'm in the music business, it goes with the territory doesn't it?'

'Simon Cowell doesn't have long hair' argued Alison.

'He's not in the music business.' Scoffed Robert who was enjoying himself now. 'The American looked like an accountant.'

'He's a lawyer actually' said Alison.

'That's even worse. You'd never trust a lawyer with long hair would you?'

For a moment it was almost like old times, Robert holding court, Lauren hanging on his every word and Alison trying to keep some sort of order. How normal it all appeared she thought and knew now why she had decided a long time ago that after divorce there ought to be an optional memory wiping process that would allow the injured party to carry on with their life.

Standing at Archie's door in the sudden dark of evening and tapping quietly, so as not to alert her ex-husband, Alison suddenly wondered if she might catch Archie and Margaret in flagrante as Lauren had done just two days before and found herself weakened by the prospect. When he answered the door he was in a state of undress and looked surprised to see her. She peered past him into the room and saw the bed was unmade.

'Sorry were you having a nap? I just wanted a quick word before we went down to dinner. There have been some developments. Shall I come in?' He hovered in the doorway looking uncomfortable and she thought she heard a noise coming from the bathroom. Vivid pictures began appearing in her head. 'It won't take a moment' she said pushing past him into the room wondering what she would do if she caught a glimpse of Margaret splashing about in the bath waiting for Archie. The thought took her back to their own watery congress and again she felt weakened. 'Actually' she stuttered, 'why don't I catch up with you in the bar in a few minutes. Don't be long though there's something I need to tell you before dinner.'

'There's no need for you to go.' He was smiling now, an Archie smile, all teeth and mouth open. 'Just got a bit of a problem in the bathroom.' He pulled the door closed and Alison's mind ventured into the 'too much information' arena.

'It's about Robert he's, well he's,' she was stuttering again.

'He's here.'

'You know?'

'Yes only just though. Nice bloke. Can I say that?'

'You can and he can be.' She paused confused by the sounds coming from the bathroom. 'So would it be alright if we had dinner together? I'm afraid Lauren invited him and I didn't feel it was right to split up the group.'

'No problem at all.' He had her arm and was walking her towards the door. 'I'll see you in the bar then, be there in a jiffy.' He deposited her on the step and closed the door. As she turned to walk away she heard voices from inside. Once again the weakened feeling returned and she had to steady herself against the tumbling bougainvillea and watch the delicate purple heads come away in her hand as she stood and listened to the hum of the American woman's voice.

FOURTEEN

'Of course it was her Lauren. Please don't ask me again if I'm sure.'

'I'm only asking because it's hard for me to believe boring old Archie's got three of you on the go over here. Bloke's turning out to be a bit of a stallion.'

'I'm beginning to wish I hadn't told you and please don't laugh, it's hardly funny.'

'Oh my God of course it's funny. Don't you get it mum? You've spent most of the week wrestling over how to tell him it's all over and you want to spent the rest of your life with John-boy and he's been shagging all over the place. Well he's really stuck it to you this time.'

'Look we'd better go, I told him I was going straight to the bar.'

'Why don't you ask him what Milva was doing in his room? There might be an easy explanation or don't you want that? You'd prefer to think of him putting out all over the place.' She stood facing her mother and blocking the door. 'We've got a tutor at college who's got an expression for moments like this. He says "it's time to shit or get off the pan".'

'Does he really' said Alison trying to move around her daughter. 'Well I can't imagine what he'd be talking about using an expression like that with young adults.'

'Final exams actually.' She stood her ground in front of her mother. 'Have you thought about talking to dad about it?' Alison looked horrified.

'Absolutely not, no and neither should you. Is that clear Lauren I don't want you to mention this to dad, I don't need his input thank you very much.'

Archie was already at the bar buying drinks for Margaret and Joan when they arrived. Alison didn't have to look at her daughter to know what she was thinking.

'Take the long way round?'

'No I just had to go back to the room for something' lied Alison. 'Did you get your bathroom sorted out?'

'What? Oh that, yes right as rain now. I see we're all here now' he said nodding in the direction of the door. Robert came towards them looking as relaxed as any visitor who might have spent the last three weeks on the island. His Hawaiian shirt was hung outside his linen trousers and he dragged his flip flops along the ground just as his daughter had done on their very first night on Nevis. His copper coloured hair was pulled back into a ponytail and Alison envied his lack of grey hairs. He looked genuinely pleased to see everyone.

'Nice shirt Bob' said Archie with real admiration.

'You can't go wrong with parrots and palm trees Archie. Keep it simple that's what I say.'

'Looks great dad.'

'If Archie had wandered into the bar in that shirt you would have been merciless in your attack on him' said Alison quietly.

'You should stop trying to defend Archie mum and accept you and him are finished. I mean if he's not copping off with the doormat over there' and she nodded towards Margaret, 'he's having a crack at Miss America.' She paused and it was the kind of pause that might have meant she was considering her mother's feelings, however Alison knew her daughter well and recognised the pause as simply the need for breath. 'Dump him before he dumps you.' Alison knew there was nothing left to say.

Robert ran the dinner table in the way he always did, with charm and humour. Alison watched as Lauren hung on his every word and Archie became invisible, a condition she had some sympathy with, being a fellow sufferer herself. It was a beautiful evening warm and clear, with just enough breeze to rustle the palm trees around the restaurant. Throughout dinner she was aware of Milva and John seated just behind them. There was no hint of how things were between them, none that she could detect anyway yet still she listened for a telling word, but there was none. Margaret and Joan had left the restaurant after eating only starters and dessert, the latter being shared between them, an unusual display of cooperation. When Maxwell suggested he serve coffee in the bar where the musicians were playing, Robert insisted they should go. They left the restaurant and Alison turned to find Milva and John's table empty and her heart sank. She knew she had spent all evening waiting to catch sight of the man she had always loved better than any other, a thought that stayed with her as she walked into the bar flanked by her ex-husband and Archie.

Milva and John were in the bar, sitting close to the band, the music so loud it was understood they wouldn't be able to speak. Lauren introduced her dad to Romeo who brought their drinks and shook hands with Robert, which seemed rather formal to Alison although her daughter seemed to like it. The jazz musicians played without vocals and the breeze pushed its way through the open shuttered windows. She noticed the music wasn't registering with Archie as it had done earlier in the holiday and she felt he had lost some of his vigour and truly hoped the appearance of Robert didn't account for that.

'There's the chap I saw earlier today, the accountant.' Robert knew very well John was a lawyer but this was Act 2 and he had his audience. Lauren laughed out loud and it improved her father's performance. 'You got an accountant Archie?'

'Not any more, sold my business a few months ago.' The drinks were taking precedence over the coffee.

'Well, when you did have one, did he look like that?' He nodded towards John.

'Jack's a lawyer, I doubt he'd be much good doing my books.'

'A Lawyer?' said Robert making it sound like it was the first time he had heard it.

'In New York and that's his wife Milva.'

'She used to be an actress' said Lauren, 'she was in Oh Calcutta!'

'Well what's a spirited woman like that doing married to him?'

'That's a very good question' said Archie quietly.

'Dad's coming to the Cook-Out tonight with me and Romeo.' Alison was barely awake as Lauren pushed back the balcony doors to let in the morning sun. 'You can come if you like but you'll probably want to bring Archie won't you?'

'Would that be so terrible?'

'He's a Loser mum.'

'Actually Lauren on his current performance he's probably the only one who isn't a Loser.'

'Whatever. I'm going to breakfast with dad, I'll see you down there but don't be long, cause he'll probably want to wait for you if he knows you're coming and I'm starving.' She was gone, leaving her mother wondering when it was their roles had swopped.

Alison knocked at Archie's door as usual but this time there was no reply and she started to wander on down to breakfast. Hummingbirds disappeared inside huge red hibiscus flower heads, their green and purple throats providing a blaze of colour as they tried to weave in and out. She wanted to be one of them, she wanted to disappear. Room service staff hung about in the gardens waiting for guests to drag themselves down to breakfast so their job could begin but until then they stretched out over their service buggies in casual conversation. She wanted to be one of them, she wanted to be among friends.

'This is Violet' Robert pulled out a chair for his ex-wife.

'I know, she's been serving us breakfast for the last week and a half.'

'Violet's daughter is away at university.' He was determined to carry on, 'and she's not very keen, is she Violet?'

'No sir, she phone me crying, "mum I'm not liking it here".' She filled their glasses steadily with iced water from a jug Alison knew she would have needed two hands to hold.

'Will you go and pick her up?' Violet shook with laughter.

'Me? I work every day so she can go to university. How can I go and pick her up? So when she aks me what to do I tell her she's got to sort this out herself.'

'And what if she can't?' asked Alison starting to feel for the child she had never met.

'Then I tell her to go pray.'

Archie didn't appear at breakfast and when Lauren took her dad for a stroll along the beach Alison decided to go back to the room the long way round. This of course meant she had to pass Margaret's room but she'd had so little exercise this holiday she felt she was justified, at least that's what she told herself. As she approached the room she could see Archie and Margaret standing in the doorway deep in conversation, Archie with his back to her. When he turned to leave Margaret stretched out to grab his hand and then threw her arms around him and for a moment Alison felt sad and excluded, not angry which is what she thought she should be feeling. Perhaps Archie had found his own true love just as she thought she had rediscovered hers a few days ago but now everything seemed to be dismantling itself around her. She needed to talk to John. She would be clever she decided and find out what she needed to know without betraying Milva's confidence or at least she would try.

'Dad's going to leave with us on Saturday. He's managed to get on our flight from St.Kitts.'

'How nice' said Alison not sounding at all like she thought it was nice. 'Has he talked to you about his new job in the States?'

'A bit' she was sheepish. 'It's okay I don't mind, I've got my exams to concentrate on and then, well maybe then I could go out there to work for a few months or even take a gap year.' It hit Alison like a bolt from the blue.

'But I thought we'd agreed you weren't going to have a gap year?'

'Things change mum, even you should realise that. Anyway nothing's settled and I doubt he's had time to mention it to the *Tooth Pick* yet.' She pulled her beach bag from underneath the bed. 'You beaching this morning?' The subject had been switched, closed and

Lauren had learned well from her fractured family.

'At some point yes but I've got a few jobs I need to do first.'

'Archie didn't come down to breakfast then?' said Lauren cramming all beach necessities into her bag until the sides began to give.

'Careful Lauren you sound concerned.' Her daughter exhaled loudly and slung the bag over her shoulder.

'You're getting me mixed up with someone who cares. See you later and if you come across my flip flops can you bring them down to the beach.'

After her daughter had left Alison had a sudden urge to pack. She pulled out her case and began selecting items to put away when there was a tap at the door. Archie was standing there holding Lauren's flip-flops.

'She left them in the restaurant and Violet gave them to me when I went down for breakfast.' He handed them over. 'You've already eaten I gather?' He sounded nervous. Alison nodded and realised she'd left him standing at the door.

'Sorry, come in won't you.'

'No I'm alright here. Thing is Ali there's something I'd like to talk to you about, are you busy this morning?' It was almost a formal request to ask if she was busy and suddenly she was back in his office, collecting papers, taking 'phone calls, being useful and it had been a long time since Alison had felt useful back then. In fact before Archie had given her a job the only thing she had felt was in the way, as though her mere presence was preventing everyone from being happy. She never tried to prevent Robert from leaving, there was no throwing herself at his feet, no screaming or crying, she just stood to one side and allowed him to go. Lauren hated her for it, believing she didn't want to fight for him, that he didn't matter to her but of course the opposite was true. She just couldn't bear to see him unhappy and being with her was making him unhappy, she knew that. Archie wasn't waiting for an answer, which was most unlike him. 'I'll see you in the car park in about thirty minutes.' She watched him walk away wondering what it was that had made him so assertive but deep inside she knew of course, it was simple, she was in the way again.

The car park was dusty and quiet and she remembered returning here a week ago after the Cook-Out. Archie had pulled her towards him telling her he had wanted her all evening and the only man she had thought about all night was John but guilt is a silent watchman.

'We've just got a quick detour to do first' he said holding open the door for her and she noticed he was bronzed now and without his usual smearing of factor fifty. 'I promised Violet I'd drop her off at the medical centre, she's got an appointment with the physio.' He started off down the road and Alison began to wonder whether she should add Violet to her list of Archie's conquests. 'It's on our way and the poor girl can hardly walk. Didn't you notice at breakfast?' She was ashamed, she hadn't noticed. 'Knee trouble.' He was laughing now and she wondered if she'd missed an innuendo in there somewhere. 'I took her earlier in the week. Oh Ali you should see the building, it's magnificent, looks more like a mansion house to me. Beautiful buildings they've got here, you must have noticed.' She stared into the distance and began to fret at how much of this holiday she had missed. 'There she is.' He sounded the horn and pulled up alongside Violet who was clearly pleased to see him.

'You don't need to go doing this I can walk.'

'I wouldn't hear of it and besides it's on our way, isn't it Ali?' Of course Alison didn't know where they were going so there was no likelihood she knew it was on their way but she smiled and lied sweetly, she could do that quite well now.

'I won't say I'm not grateful, it makes the journey much easier for me.' She spread herself across the back seat of the car and lifted her knee. 'The physiotherapist say I'm making good progress but I can't say I agree with her.' She began laughing and changed the whole atmosphere in the car with the simple toleration of her suffering. 'You going to Cook-Out again tonight?'

'I don't know, what do you think Ali, shall we give it another go?' She took his words and dissected them in her head giving them a whole new meaning, "shall we give it another go?" She felt she had lost him now and, given the chance, she would have very much liked to "give it another go" but she knew it was over. He had become polite with her now, all familiarity had disappeared, she had lost him but to what or to whom, she didn't know.

The medical centre was a wide, low building with steps leading up to the main door. Opposite was a nursing home and Alison could see people sitting in the garden and being wheeled in chairs around the flowerbeds. The pale yellow building contrasted beautifully with the vivid blue sky and the woodwork around the rails was so delicate it was hard to believe someone might have conceived this as a place where people could be put back together again. There was much thanking on the part of Violet and she disappeared into a small door on the ground floor, glad she didn't have to negotiate the steps.

'There's something I want to show you' he said, 'it's not far from here. In fact I came across it last week when I brought Violet down here.' They drove for another few minutes and then pulled off the main road onto a dirt track lined with small dwellings, some shack-like, others looking like they were half built. The gardens were littered with cars, mostly looking like scrap and one serving as a chicken coop. They drove to the end and Archie parked the car. As they got out a mother duck led her ducklings across the road in front of them in a perfect line until they reached the shrubbery where, like children out of school, they ran aimlessly in every direction.

They were facing a small chattel house surrounded by a low fence that now formed part of the overgrown garden. The roof had dislodged and was at an angle with the rest of the building and a small banana tree had grown up through the roof space creating an attractive contrast with the corrugated iron. One of the walls was missing entirely and most of the windows were out. Archie turned to Alison and beamed.

'This is it Ali, my very own chattel house.' He was triumphant.

'This is yours?' Incredulous.

'It will be as soon as the paperwork's completed.' He held back the gate so she could enter. 'I'm going to be an Alien Landholder Ali, what do you think of that?'

'I think the whole thing's alien Archie. Are you mad?' He looked crestfallen. 'What I mean is how will this all work, how will you manage things from home?' Then it struck her, she was looking at Archie's new home.

'There's a lovely bench in the back garden, let's go and talk.' He took her hand and led her around the house. It was built on bricks and had all the hallmarks of a fine chattel house like so many on the island. Each of the remaining windows was shuttered and inside the layout was simple but she could see how it might easily be made into a home with just a caring hand and very little imagination, both of which qualified Archie for the task.

'I'm sorry to be so negative but it seems a huge job.'

'Those are the kinds of jobs Archie likes.' He turned his face away from her in the way people do when they have something difficult to say. Just as Robert had done when he told her he would be leaving, in fact that part he did face to face but when it came to the fact he was about to be a father again, he looked away. How strange, she had always thought, that he was able to look her in the eye and say that twenty years of devotion had come to an end but when it came to the baby he couldn't face her.

'Look at me.' She turned his face around towards her. 'Look at me Archie, what's going on here? Can't you just talk to me? You see I've been surrounded by lies for so long I'm tired now and to be honest, I'd just like to know the truth.'

FIFTEEN

'Being on my own after mother died took a lot of getting used to and I'm sorry if that sounds lame but I'd never lived on my own before. It wasn't that she was against my marrying but I never seemed to get round to it with the business to run and then when she became ill I seemed to spend any spare time I had making sure she was comfortable. I never knew my father so it was always just me and her you see. We had our little routine, I'd get home, she'd cook dinner and we'd talk and I know that probably sounds small to you Ali but I liked that. I liked her, we were friends. I really missed her when she died but then you came along and sort of filled that gap.'

'Actually I never saw myself as a surrogate mother.'

'Archie didn't mean that.' He took her hand again, 'but we talked you and me, you seemed interested in what I had to say and not many people are interested in what Archie has to say.' He placed her hand carefully on the bench and the disconnection registered with her so she waited. 'So when you became a bigger part of my life I couldn't believe my luck. You're beautiful, intelligent, all those things every man wants but most settle for less. I knew Lauren didn't like me, well she still doesn't but I wanted to try with her and I'm not sorry she came on holiday, although I could have done without the teasing.' She waited for him to go on, wishing all the time she hadn't hurt this sensitive man. 'Anyway it's been a great holiday for me because I discovered this' and he waved his arm at the house. 'I know you can't see it Ali but to me it represents a rebuilding of things and I can lose myself in a project like this and be really happy.'

'But Archie I thought you were happy at home, that's why you wanted to retire?'

'I wanted to retire to spend more time with you but that's not going to happen is it?' She hated his direct question that forced her into facing up to what was between them. 'Come on Ali it's not just you who wants the truth?' She felt backed into a corner.

'And what do you want Archie, apart from this house I mean?

Because I don't think you want me and don't think I haven't noticed how friendly you and Margaret have become.' He smiled. 'And not just Margaret either.' She was on a roll. 'Who was in your room last night when I called?' The smiled disappeared.

'I don't want to talk about that.'

'Christ Archie I know who it was, I heard you talking. It was Milva, Archie I know that but why can't you tell me?'

'It's private.'

'Private? Well it wasn't so private when she kissed you on your patio the other evening because I saw that Archie, I bloody well saw that.'

'I've made you angry and I didn't mean to do that. I just wanted to show you this house and tell you what I was up to.....' She jumped in.

'I know what you're up to Archie I'm just not sure who with.' He got up, walked towards the car and waited for her. They didn't speak again.

'Well I think it'll be much better without Archie there, getting down with the locals, he's embarrassing.' Lauren shook out her swimsuit and laid it over the balcony. 'Bit of a shocker him buying the house though. I mean it's a bit adventurous for him isn't it? Like I thought Captain Thunderbolt shorts was about as exciting as he got. I'm surprised he wants all that work at his age.'

'At his age?' Alison was astonished, 'he's not that much older than your father Lauren.'

'Yeah but dad's cool and he's not up for retirement yet is he, I mean he's just gone and got himself another job in the music industry.'

'As a consultant.'

'So is a consultant what people become when they're too old to get a proper job?'

Alison knew her daughter was being deliberately naive and refused to rise to the bait. Robert was showing no signs of wanting to retire or even slow down but then he did have his new young family to consider. Archie however had been looking forward to his retirement for some time even though he loved what he did. She never understood why he wanted to sell his company it had always been the adhesive in his life. It was the one thing that had joined everything else together but now that he seemed to be moving back in that direction Alison realised it was she who had been deliberately naive. He was no longer seeing her as part of his future, she was no longer that important to him. Now she was being replaced by a rundown chattel house which she felt was probably preferable to an over-zealous forty-something carer or an American whose marriage was all but over. Strange though that when they were at the house today he wouldn't talk about either of them. It had made her unhappy that there were too many questions left unanswered.

The Cook-Out had been the perfect forum for Robert to expand his personal skills with the locals. Alison was surprised at how well he still danced and how much in demand he seemed to be with the young women who called to him from behind the barbeques, waving a long fork as they turned the chicken, spitting and browning. The music was deafening which was just the way he liked it and she had to admit he was fitting in very well. She could see Lauren was proud and her face glowed like an over-bearing parent on Speech Day. Alison had never been able to tell her daughter how much Robert had hurt her, in some ways she pretended he hadn't, always trying to carry on as usual as he moved out of their lives and into his new arena where he was openly loved. Always loved, that was Robert, there always seemed to be someone available to love him: Lauren, his new, fashionable, young wife, the twins and now he was the toast of the Cook-Out. Some men had it all.

Robert had insisted they walk back to the hotel after Lauren and Romeo had disappeared in search of *Killer Bee* cocktails and although she would have preferred a taxi Alison deferred to him. Such habits were hard to break.

'A couple of the locals were asking where the "guy with the happy face" was tonight. I take it they were referring to Archie?'

'They must have been.'

'Sounds like he had a good time last week, why didn't he show tonight?' He was being casual but she sensed where the conversation was going.

'I don't know why he's not here, you'll have to ask him.'

'Or ask Lauren.' He was smiling and she waited for the intrusion into her private life. 'Sorry but you know our daughter can't keep a secret.' She did know, in fact Lauren's idea of keeping a secret was only telling one person at a time. 'You've had a long face all night, what's up? I thought you and Archie were close?'

'Stop playing with me Robert, you know what's up. How much has Lauren told you?' He didn't have to open his mouth for her to realise he knew everything. She stopped walking and for a few seconds he continued to walk away from her and she wanted to run while his back was turned, to run and just keep running. He turned around. 'Don't make yourself miserable over this. Talk to me.'

'God you're so bloody conceited. You really think that don't you, that if I talk over my problems with you they will all go away, that somehow you will make things better?'

'I'm sorry, I'm sorry' he backed away from her, 'I just thought you might appreciate talking it through with another grown-up instead of dumping it all on our daughter.' For a moment she thought she might hit him. Alison hadn't ever hit anyone in her life but suddenly it seemed possible and just hours after she wanted to tip him over her balcony. Was it him or was it her, she asked herself.

'My God if you want to talk about dumping stuff on our daughter you could teach me a thing or two. In fact only a few days ago I was asked to tell her you'd be moving your new family out of her life and to the States. Don't lecture me about dumping on our daughter you're the fucking master at screwing up people's lives.'

'That's true I am.' He had surprised her with his reply. Robert being contrite was unheard of in Alison's experience. 'I did screw things up at home big-time and I'm sorry I ever did that. Of course that doesn't mean to say I'm through with screwing things up, I've got a whole new family to work on now.'

'Is that supposed to make me feel sorry for you or them?'

'Neither really, it's not your problem anymore.' They started to walk back to the hotel. 'You never mentioned a John when you used to talk about your time in New York.' There, he had said his name and she had never wanted that. She didn't want it out in public like they might be talking about just anyone. They were about to pass another Cook-Out at the side of the road, all lit up in orange and yellow against the dark night sky. Here the food seemed secondary to the music and dancing and she wanted to lose herself in amongst the easy laughter and the apparent ease of the locals. 'Have you made up your mind what you're going to do yet?'

She wanted to say, well actually I had decided I wanted to be with John, he was always the love of my life, not like you, you shit, who hurt me and pushed me around until I felt insignificant and worthless. Then two days ago I found out he had been screwing me around just as much as you ever did and the only man who has come out of all this mess with any honour is Archie but unfortunately he seems to be having relationships with half the tourists on the island at the moment. Oh and he's buying a house here so he's moving out of my life anyway. But instead she just replied, 'No, not yet' because it was simple and true.

They had a drink in the bar when they got back to the hotel and Archie was in there with Margaret and probably for the first time, her mother was not in attendance. They waved when they first went in but Robert steered her to the bar and pulled up a couple of stools as he ordered their drinks. He had taken a packet of cigarettes out of his pocket and was playing with them, turning the packet over and over but making no attempt at opening it. They both sat and focused on the repeated movement as though it were the cabaret that permitted them not to speak. A saxophone burst into life behind them and the cigarette packet became dormant as they turned towards the music. She had a clear view of Archie, now deep in conversation with the new Margaret in her flowing dress and bronzed skin, her hair pulled back from her face and held in place with a hair band. Alison suddenly felt invisible and she had spent a lot of time over the last few years working on that feeling. In fact it was Archie who had helped give her the confidence to rediscover herself. It was Archie who had given her a job, a reason to get out of bed in the morning. It was Archie who had made the hurt go away after her divorce. It had all been about Archie, he had saved her life and she had never said thank you.

'You're staring at him' said Robert without looking at her. 'If you're that bothered why don't we go over and sit with them? He's far too polite to gate-crash our party.'

She mulled over her ex-husband's words, "polite". She had never thought of Archie as being particularly polite but then she had never thought of Archie being anything except dear Archie. Although he never did press her when she was troubled about her divorce, or insist they talk about Lauren's rudeness towards him. He had almost always just left her to her own thoughts until she decided she wanted to talk and then he was there, he had always been there. She was realising, very quickly now, that she could no longer rely on him to be there and worse than that, she could no longer call him her dear Archie. Margaret was hanging on his every word, her small mouth, over-filled with teeth, breaking into a smile when he paused for breath. Alison watched as the woman who was replacing her carefully folded her hands on her lap so as not to crease her dress and crossed her feet, one sandal over the other beneath her skirts. Robert got off his stool and took her arm.

'We're going over to sit with them.' She snatched her arm away.

'I'm not going.'

'Yes you are.' He stood in front of her, his back to Archie and playmate. 'Look it was you he came on holiday with and unless he's told you, which I don't think he has, that he doesn't want to see you any more, then we should join them and try and carry on as normal.'

'I'm not sure what normal is.'

'It'll be alright, trust me.' He approached Margaret with his hand out and introduced himself, neatly moving her away from Archie allowing his ex-wife to sit down. When Robert started a conversation it could be about almost anything, politics, wine, football but never music, never the thing he knew most about. It would always be his way to leave himself exposed in discussion so that he might fumble his way around the topic making difficult points with apparent innocence. Alison sat tight waiting for Archie to speak but the silence was long as it had been in the car that afternoon. She searched for something to say and envied Robert and his linguistic expertise. Then, like her ex-husband, she chose to leave herself exposed in discussion.

'Did you have dinner with Margaret this evening?'

'She and Joan invited me to share their table. How was the Cook-Out?'

'Great fun.' She said with ridiculous enthusiasm.

'That good?' He seemed to be half smiling. 'Did you see Milva and John on your travels, I think they went along this evening?' He took her hesitation as a 'no' and continued, 'ah well there's more than one event of course. You wouldn't necessarily have seen them.'

'No, it would seem I'm very much outside the circle this evening. In fact I'm not sure I can even tell you where my daughter is at this very moment.'

'She's over there' he nodded towards the bar as Lauren and Romeo walked in. 'You didn't come back together then?'

'What are you suggesting?' she hissed, 'that my ex and I wandered off together for some reason?'

'Ali I'm not suggesting anything, really I'm not. Look I'm quite tired this evening and I've got a lot to do tomorrow, things to finalise on the house before I leave. I'm going to have an early night.' He was walking away from her before she had collected her thoughts sufficiently to open her mouth. Margaret shot out of her seat at the sight of him leaving and they walked towards the door together and Alison imagined he put his arm around her and pulled her towards him, but he didn't, he simply put his head down and kept walking, away from her, just as men who really mattered to her always did. Then there they sat, she and Robert. He on one side of the table and her on the other, then he shook his head.

'Well you got that wrong, they aren't having an affair at all.

He's been helping her, not helping himself you silly girl.'

'I don't understand.'

'She just told me. Apparently her mother has been hankering to move in with her because she can't manage the stairs in her own house and Archie has been arranging, through a builder mate of his who lives close by, to fit a stair lift so the old dragon can stay put. Christ she sounds like a right handful this Joan but Margaret says your man's been nothing short of wonderful and given her her life back.'

'Yes he does that Archie, gives people their lives back.'

'She said they were kindred spirits as he looked after his mother for years and understood how it can take over your life.'

'Still doesn't explain the tumble in the bedroom Lauren claims to have seen.'

'Well reading between the lines she did hint at being a little over zealous with her gratitude but she said he was the perfect gentleman throughout, so nothing for you to worry about on that score it would seem.'

'That would be typical of Archie, if she did make a fool of herself, he would never embarrass her or break a confidence.'

'You should talk to him.'

'I will tomorrow.'

'That's right don't go doing anything spontaneous like rushing after him and telling him you got it all wrong eh?'

'I leave spontaneity to you.'

SIXTEEN

'This time tomorrow morning we'll be leaving the island for home.' Lauren was sitting up in bed. 'I'm going to miss Nevis.'

'Nevis or Romeo?' Alison pushed open the balcony doors in her morning ritual to bring the daylight into the room. 'I didn't hear you come in last night.'

'I thought you were pretending to be asleep. John and Milva were at the Cook-Out, did you see them?'

'No, dad and I walked back.'

'They didn't look like they were having a particularly good time if that makes you feel any better.'

'It doesn't but thanks anyway.'

'So you haven't had a chance to speak to him yet then?'

'I've only seen him in passing since the power cut.'

'No change there then' she laughed. 'Let's face it mum the last time the lights went out you didn't see him for over thirty years, so if you get lucky it might be another thirty.'

'I've decided I'm going to ask him about Geena today.'

'I thought you didn't want to break Milva's confidence although I don't know why, it's not like you owe her anything is it?'

'I suppose it's because I feel like I've lost everything too now, just like her. I don't expect Archie and I will continue seeing each other when we get home, it seems pretty much over and I certainly won't be starting my new life with John will I, not if Milva's version of events is to be believed.'

'You're asking him about Geena because you want him to say something to make you change your mind. You still want to be with him don't you?'

'How did you get such a wise old head on those young shoulders?'

'Don't go backwards mum, he's a shit and you know he is. How long would it be before he shafted you just like he did Milva? You really know how to pick them mum, even Archie's turned into a monster womaniser.'

'Actually he hasn't, well not with Margaret anyway. I found out last night the reason for their secret little chats. Archie's been arranging for a builder friend of his to have a look at Joan's house and do the necessary work so that she can stay on there a bit longer. You know she's been insisting she can't cope on her own and needs to move in with Margaret, so the idea is to make the house a bit more Joan-friendly.'

'Sounds like a contradiction in terms.'

'Quite but the whole thing's been top secret otherwise Joan might scupper the idea and move in with Margaret anyway.

'There's still the Milva thing that's been going on.'

'True but that matters less to me in some ways.'

'Why because you and John were fuck-buddies while she was getting measured for her wedding dress?'

'A beautiful turn of phrase.'

'It doesn't matter how you want to tart it up mum, he's bad news and you know it, even dad said he could tell he was a rat.'

'Yes thanks for discussing my private life with your father, just what I needed.'

'I'm sorry but he knew there was something up with you and I honestly thought he could help.'

'Did he really say he thought John was a rat?'

'A *fucking rat* actually but you know how I hate to swear.'

Although it was John she was looking for, it was Milva that Alison came across first, stretched out on the sun lounger in front of her room. She was lying on her front and reading and Alison could easily have walked by without being noticed but she hovered and spoke her name. The American turned over and lifted her sunglasses.

'Oh it's you' then she turned back to her book, 'you looking for someone?'

'Not especially I just wondered if you'd seen Archie go down to breakfast?' she lied. 'Or perhaps Robert?'

'My oh my what a lucky girl you are, two men to chose from. I haven't seen either of them but,' she flung her book across the grass and stood up to face her, 'Jack is here,' she called over her shoulder into the room while all the time fixing her gaze on Alison, 'hey Jack you want breakfast? Ali's asking.'

'I wasn't asking actually.' She was very uncomfortable now and turned to walk away just as John emerged. She had hardly seen him over the last few days and found she could barely take her eyes off him.

'I'll walk down to breakfast with you. My wife's not eating today.' He was moving quickly as if in a rush to get away.

'Did you hear that Ali? I'm not eating today.' Alison was waiting for permission to leave but she wasn't sure Milva had given it. She looked at John, he shook his head and nodded they should go. She had permission now. 'You two have a good time why don't you. No need to rush back.'

They didn't speak until they reached breakfast and only after John had found them a table outside by the water's edge. It made a pleasant change she thought from the table adjacent to the buffet which always seemed to be Archie's first choice and she welcomed pleasant changes this morning.

'Why isn't Milva eating?'

'She's on hunger strike.'

'It's a serious question, is she felling unwell?'

'Not unwell no, just pissed with me. I must have done something, God knows what, although I don't know why she took a piece out of you this morning.'

'I think I might know why she's angry.'

'Enlighten me.' He seemed hardly interested and called the waitress to order.

'Let me ask you something else first.' This was it, the moment she had played out in her mind over the last days, she'd planned it, word for word. Then she realised what a waste of time her preparation had been, as usual. 'Why did Michael 'phone me to finish our relationship and not you?'

'That's a funny question after all these years.' He looked genuinely shocked at her question and with that came a certain innocence she wanted to latch on to but she knew she had to let him go on, and bury himself. 'The answer is I'm not sure I can remember. I think we just decided it was better you and I weren't in touch any more. Milva had discovered our affair and you know how things were back then.' He moved the cutlery around the table. 'I think Michael was worried I wouldn't be able to finish it with you and so he offered to do it. Hell I can't remember.' She knew he was lying but still she loved him. Even as his mouth moved around every twisted word she wanted to pull him towards her and kiss him, forgiving everything. 'Isn't it where we find ourselves today that's most important?'

'And where do we find ourselves today?'

'Together, that's where, together for Christ's sake. We both know this is the right thing, the thing that should have happened all those years ago. I wish I had 'phoned you because I don't think I could have finished it myself.' He reached across the table and grabbed her hand making her tremble. 'We need to put the past behind us and be together.'

'I'm not sure I can put the past behind us.'

'It's history, let it go.'

'Lauren says it's our history that makes us what we are today.'

'I'll let you know when I want to take advice from your daughter. Did she have any other words of wisdom for her mother?' He was getting irritated with her. 'Come on we don't need some kid to light the way for us, not at our age.'

'She's not "some kid", she's my daughter and if we do spend time together she will certainly be part of that.'

'Oh what like she's made it such a great holiday for Archie by beating him up every chance she gets? Although I do get where she's coming from on that one.'

'Actually she's not particularly complimentary about you either.' He shook his head as though he disbelieved her but she wouldn't argue with him. She didn't know a great deal about matters of the heart but supposed it was possible to find someone both wonderful and detestable at the same time. Perhaps that's what real love was, a combination of both these things. Perhaps that's why true love survived everything because it knew everything. There was a sound behind them and Robert pulled up a chair and sat down.

'Have you ordered yet?' He picked up the menu. 'Our daughter tells me the pumpkin pancakes are out of this world.' He smiled at his ex-wife and the use of "our daughter" registered with her first and then with John as he relaxed his grip on her hand. A stake had been placed in the ground dividing the table. 'So what's everyone up to today, last day for us.' She heard him being inclusive again. 'What about you Jack or should I call you John?' It was the final blow that said he knew all and his knowledge weakened John who got up quietly and left the table. Alison stared at the empty chair and the rearranged cutlery and had the urge to replace each item as though he had never been there.

'I hear dad saw John off at breakfast.' They were walking down to the beach.

'You make it sound like a dog fight.'

'Clever though, dad I mean. You must still like him mum, dad I mean.'

‘I know who you mean Lauren.’

‘So did you get the answers you wanted from John before dad showed up?’

‘I asked him the question and he lied.’

‘I hope you told him you knew he was lying to you?’

‘That part wasn’t important to me any longer.’

‘I’d have told him, I wouldn’t want him to think he’d made a fool out of me.’

‘Something you might learn as you get older daughter dear is that a person knowing they’ve made a fool of you is often not as important as you simply knowing it. I know he’s made a fool of me Lauren, I don’t need him to know too.’

They had stayed on the beach until the sun went down when Robert produced a tray of spectacular looking cocktails and they sat and sipped in silence. They had spent all day together, the three of them, mum, dad and daughter, looking very ordinary to any passers-by. Alison felt the last few days had been a healing process for Lauren who had become as close to her father now as she had been as a small child. How strange it was that the holiday that was always known as “Archie’s treat” had been responsible for so many changes to so many lives, not least his own. Archie had been busy all day completing paperwork for the purchase of the chattel house and Alison hadn’t been expecting to see him but now just as the sun was disappearing beyond the dark blue ocean he joined them on the beach. He was already dressed for dinner and gone were the loud swimming shorts and crazy t-shirts and Alison doubted she would ever see them again. Robert seemed genuinely pleased to see him and even Lauren had a civil word, which, strangely, made Alison feel rather uncomfortable. It was a pleasant gathering and when Robert and Lauren got up to leave Archie asked her to stay behind with him. She asked him if all legal work had been completed on the house and when he answered her he was composed and steady, no longer the funny man trying to fill every gap with familiarities. It seemed he had somehow grown-up, come of age in the last few days or perhaps not so much grown-up as grown away from her.

'I'll need to come back soon and finish up a few bits and pieces but that's no problem I'm going to have plenty of time on my hands now and Violet's going to keep an eye on things for me until then.' Alison remembered the lovely Violet whose troubled daughter was told to "go pray" for parental guidance, her busy mother working hard to support her. 'So, if you ever feel like a trip back to Nevis let me know, of course you might have to do a bit of brick laying when you get here.' There it was, just a little joke to take the edge off the awkwardness of the conversation. 'Anyway I've booked us all a rail table for dinner so shall I see you in the bar, in about an hour?'

'I heard about the good work you've been doing with Margaret for her mother's house.' He looked a little embarrassed. 'I'm sorry I misjudged you on that.' She didn't go on to say, *oh and there's the small matter of Milva I'd like you to clear up*, because now she didn't think it would ever be cleared up, there wouldn't be the time.

'I understand Margaret' he said 'what I mean is I understand her predicament. Not unlike mine for many years, looking after an ageing parent but her situation is much worse. You must have noticed how difficult Joan can make things for her.' She was surprised by his clear understanding of the problem, his compassion and caring and yet she knew they should be no surprise to her really. 'Anyway hopefully we have solved her problem or at least put off the possibility of Joan moving in with her for a little while yet. She said she didn't know how to thank me.' Alison wanted to say *I heard she did* but said nothing because she'd said too much already. They went their separate ways, he to the bar and she towards her room.

When she arrived she could see Archie's cases had already been packed and were just inside his window. The curtains to Milva's room were drawn and all was quiet there. Upstairs Lauren had showered and dressed and was about to leave to meet up with Romeo before dinner. She seemed upbeat and Alison decided her father's appearance had probably smoothed the forthcoming separation from the handsome, young West Indian boy. In fact her daughter looked happy and relaxed, not a state Lauren very often enjoyed. Her short, white, strapless dress had been kept until the last evening to celebrate her glowing suntan. The flip flops had been replaced with killer heels in royal blue and her hair was pulled back from her face and twisted at the back of her neck.

Alison thought she looked quite beautiful.

'Don't be late to the restaurant. Archie's booked our table and it is our last evening so we should all be there.'

'I wouldn't miss it for the world' she smiled and disappeared out of the door.

She hadn't expected Robert to call for her but she was glad to see him when she opened the door. He was as ever cool, relaxed and looking for fun and for a moment she was saddened by the fact they had been unable to stay together and then realised it was simply because he was cool, relaxed and always looking for fun.

'You look stunning as ever' he said without looking at her as she picked her way through the gardens to the deafening sound of the night time frogs. There was a slight breeze but it was warm and the air was heavy with the strong scent of frangipani as they neared the bar, yellow and bright and humming with the sound of saxophones. Robert's ears seemed to prick up. 'I love it here, in fact I wish I could commute to the States from Nevis, it's a paradise. Your man's got the right idea about buying a house here.'

'I'm not sure he's my man anymore.'

'Says who, you or Archie?'

'Too much has happened over the last ten days to go back to the way we were.'

'But why would you want to do that, go back to the way you were? Perhaps where you are now is better than that?'

'Trouble is I don't know where I am. John's a liar and a cheat and won't change and my lovely daughter now tells me she might want to take a gap year in the States with you.'

'Come on now' he interrupted her, 'that was just an idea nothing's firm about any of that.' That meant he hadn't asked his new wife thought Alison. 'And what about Archie?'

'He's got his project, his plan for the future and he's changed towards me. He's more controlled now. I can't explain he's just different that's all.'

'Different isn't always so bad.'

They went in to dinner and their table was set in the middle of the balcony. It was an elegant restaurant and Alison could see why people might insist on a rail table. Nowhere else in the room afforded such a view of the gardens, the ocean and the sky and tonight all three looked magnificent. Maxwell was waiting for them and Alison did a quick count of the place settings, not just four places but twice as many, they were to be joined for dinner.

SEVENTEEN

Milva's voice rang out across the restaurant.

'Great table Archie and it's going to be some cabaret tonight.' Alison wondered what she meant. 'We've got a hell of a view' she said nodding towards the stars. She looked a little strained and Alison wondered if she was regretting confiding in her about John and she recognised that emotion, it was regret. Margaret and Joan arrived with the least fuss she had ever seen and she noticed Joan seemed less reliant on her sticks and Alison wondered if it was Nevis or Archie who had magic healing powers. They were waiting for Lauren just as they had done on the first night of the holiday.

'I'll sit beside you until Lauren gets here' said Archie 'but then I'll move so she can enjoy the view one last time with you.'

'I'm not sure young girls have much time for such things these days' said Joan already mischievous.

'Unless that view happens to include a good looking barman' shouted Milva.

'I'm sure I wouldn't know about that.'

'I'm sure you wouldn't' replied Milva and it was hard to judge just who was spitting more poison.

By the time Lauren arrived everyone had ordered but Robert had already chosen for his daughter. However, the idea his actions might make her entrance transparent was faintly ridiculous to Alison as chairs were moved and Archie took up residence next to Margaret producing a very smug smile from Joan.

'Sorry, sorry we got held up' whispered Lauren to her mother as she sat down.

'Never mind you're here now. Where have you been?'

'Actually Romeo took me over to look at the house Archie's

bought.'

'I didn't realise it was common knowledge.'

'Violet is Romeo's aunt.'

'I'm still not sure why he would take you there.'

'He thought I might be interested.'

'Sorry Lauren but why exactly? Why might you be interested in Archie's house I mean you can't bear the poor man, why did you go?'

'I didn't want to disappoint him, Romeo that is not Archie of course.'

'Of course and what did you think?'

'I liked it actually. It's sort of Archie if that makes sense.'

'What old and falling apart you mean?'

'Mum.'

'Don't "mum" me Lauren you're the one who's been nipping at his ankles all holiday.'

'You know what, I think you've got a real problem with age and if you want the truth I think he will probably make a good job of doing it up. It's his thing isn't it, building and stuff. You've just got to look at other chattel houses on the island to see how lovely it might look. You know you're not being very supportive mum.'

'Lauren you are kidding me aren't you?' A smile crept over her daughter's face. 'I think you've got a separate agenda in all this and it might be something to do with that young man over there.' Romeo was bringing drinks to their table and saving his brilliant smile for her daughter. 'You're going to miss him I think.'

'Not if we pop back from time to time to check out Archie's building project.'

'Hang on a minute I'm beginning to think all roads lead to Romeo here.' Alison thought her daughter flushed a little and decided not to press her but instead enjoy the fact that for tonight, at least, Lauren seemed to have lost her brittle edge. Returning to the island to see Archie wouldn't be possible, that was over now but she couldn't ignore the fact that this afternoon he had suggested she might like to come back and see how his project was progressing. Perhaps this was just politeness thought Alison but there was something about his offer that made it seem he was still interested in her. Now she must decide whether she was still interested in him.

They were the last to leave the restaurant, called to the bar by the music and promises of dancing. At the table they had all followed instructions to be seated but in the bar they were thrown against a cluster of sofas in the corner without the comfort of buffer states. Lauren took to the floor with Robert, Archie and Margaret joined them at Joan's insistence and John sat next to Alison.

'I've been wanting to talk to you all night, you look fabulous by the way.' Alison cringed at his use of "by the way", as if the compliment was an aside, or an unimportant addition and she felt that "by the way" was no more sophisticated than Archie's employment of levity. 'I'm going to miss you.' She said nothing. 'When I get back to the States I'll put the wheels in motion, tell Milva what's going on,' he threw back his head and swallowed his drink. 'Then I'm going to get on the first 'plane back to the UK to be with you.' He put the glass to his lips again.

'You've finished it' she said.

'What?' he was confused. 'My drink you mean, yes I have haven't I.'

'Well I didn't mean your marriage.'

'I've told you before, it's over, it has been over for some time. The only thing I want now is to be with you.' She was close to him now, as close as she had been to him at the very first Calypso Night when she could feel the heat from his body. Tonight, at long last, she could feel nothing towards him. Perhaps a little indifference and maybe pity but the passion had left her now. He reached down and touched her hand. 'I can't believe we're going to be together again at last.' She pulled her hand away and noticed Archie had been watching them from the dance floor but his face told her nothing. She became tired with the deceit.

'She knows John, Milva knows.'

'About what? You and me? Has that bloody daughter of yours said something? I told you I wanted to sort this out my way.' He had become red faced and she didn't care for him with a red face and she certainly didn't care for the way he spoke about Lauren.

'Not about you and me. About you and Geena.' She looked away when she told him and thought afterwards she shouldn't have done that because there are few pleasures greater in life than knowing a person is about to get what's coming to them and one of those is actually seeing them get it. If she had looked she would have seen him open and close his mouth several times and all the blood drain from his red face. 'She can't?'

'Not denying it then?' Still looking away.

'Absolutely I'm denying it. Geena? This is complete rubbish.'

'She told me the other night, on the beach, the night of the power-cut. How is it significant things always seem to happen to me when the lights go out?' She paused to give him the opportunity to speak but he said nothing. 'Geena told her just before you two left for Nevis. She told her about the affair you are currently having and she also told her about the affair you were having' and now she turned to look at him, 'while you were having your affair with me, all those years ago' and she saw he understood her.

'Oh for Christ's sake.' He ran his hands through his hair and looked vulnerable and suddenly it meant nothing to her. He spoke in a whisper. 'But why would she tell you?'

'I don't know John, perhaps it's because you're such a complete bastard she can't talk to you.'

'I don't know what to say.'

'There is one thing you can tell me. Why was it Michael 'phoned me to say we couldn't meet again, why didn't you do it? Was it because you could barely speak after he beat you up that night?' She had to check herself to be sure she wasn't making excuses for him because she wanted this to be over.

'Michael never really forgave me for stealing you away from him.

'Don't be ridiculous, he had Geena.'

'That's true but they hadn't been together long and I think he was still smarting from breaking up with you. Then he gets home and finds I'm involved with girlfriend number two and I think he just snapped.'

'He found you in bed with her.'

'Yes okay, I did a terrible thing. I'm sorry, I wish I hadn't done it. What do you want me to say?'

'I want you to tell me why Michael 'phoned me.'

'He said you needed to be rid of me, that I was no good for you. He knew that if I 'phoned you it wouldn't end. He couldn't trust me to do that but he knew you well enough to know that if he made the call it would be finished. That it would hurt you enough to make you walk away. I guess he was still looking out for you.'

'That makes me feel very sad. I really liked Michael.'

'Yes, so did I.'

'Really? I'm not sure you've ever cared deeply about anyone.'

She hadn't noticed but Robert had appeared at their table, he held out his hand.

'Would the lady care to dance?' As she stood up John pulled at her arm.

'We can't leave it like this, I've so many questions for you.' Robert leant over and brushed away his hand.

'You do know there are more questions than answers John. I would have thought a bright Accountant like you would have known that.'

'You told him then?' They were dancing and he was holding her close and she tried to ignore the fact she was glad he was there.

'It didn't give me any pleasure.'

'Liar.'

'He just sat there so smug I couldn't stop myself. God I hope I haven't made things worse for Milva, I wouldn't want to do that.

'I expect you've done her a favour.'

'I doubt that.'

All evening the music had filled the bar. The deep full tone of the saxophones seemed to bridge gaps between the tables and allowed people to move around more freely. When at last it stopped everything was laid bare, the alcohol, the dancers, the mood was changed. So as the saxophonists packed away their instruments and the drum kit was disabled so were the guests. With promises that this wasn't goodbye, that would take place tomorrow at breakfast so deferring the final curtain, everyone departed for their rooms. All the staff had left and Alison took a detour and wandered into the restaurant.

The tables had been cleared and reset for the next evening and when the guests came in and took their places she would be thirty thousand miles above the Atlantic Ocean on her way home. There were no candles lit but the small white lights still burned bright along the balcony and the sky was crowded with stars. Alison pulled out a chair at the rail table and took a seat, just as she had done on the first night they had arrived when everything had been before her. She replayed the events of the last ten days in her mind and tried not to dwell on those things she might have changed. It had been a momentous few days and she had fallen in love with Nevis but fallen out of love with John, after all these years.

'There's no doubt, this is the best table in the restaurant.' Milva sat down beside her. 'You know why I like a rail table Ali? It's not just because it's the best table in the room, it's not just because it gives you the best view. The reason I want it Ali is because everyone else wants it.'

'I'm not sure we shou d be in here.' It was a lame try at excusing herself.

'I've spent most of my life being in places I shouldn't be. Don't get up, let's enjoy the night sky. Do you know anything about astronomy?' Alison didn't reply. 'Me neither but what's that thing called where people see random shapes in clouds or sand or something?' She brushed her hair back from her face in the way that John often did and Alison wondered if perhaps it was true that after many years of being together people did begin to ape one another.

'Pareidolia.'

'What d'you say?'

'It's called Pareidolia.'

'Yeah that's it, where people say they can see the face of the Virgin Mary in the top of a cappuccino, that kind of thing.' She laughed and Alison wondered if she was simply amusing herself. 'Take a look at that sky Ali, what can you see up there?'

'Stars.'

'I thought you had more imagination than that.'

'Why would I want to trick my brain into seeing something that's not really there?'

'Same reason you might want to tell yourself something is true when you know it's a darn lie. You must have done that.'

'Once maybe, but no longer. You only end up kidding yourself.'

'Yep and it's a long hike back to reality.'

'I really must go, I've got to finish my packing.'

'I know about you and Jack.' Her words hit like a hammer. 'I know he was screwing you when he was engaged to me and I know he's screwing you again now but hell Ali, who *isn't* Jack screwing?' Her eyes were filled with tears and Alison wanted to reach out to her but knew she had no right, 'and guess what, I've told Archie.' This second bombshell echoed around her head for a few moments before the realisation of it all struck her. So Archie knew, after all her attempts at keeping it from him, he knew. 'It wasn't the first conversation I'd had with him about Jack. He knew we weren't getting along, although he didn't know why.'

'When did you tell him?' She wasn't sure why she'd asked that question. Archie knowing was bad enough and finding out exactly how long he'd known for wasn't going to help but she asked anyway.

'When you came to Archie's room the other night, I was in the middle of telling him.'

'That's dreadful.'

'What is, you turning up in the middle of things or me telling him?'

'Both.'

'Well I think that puts us more or less even now don't you?'

'I doubt that but why tell Archie, why didn't you confront me?'

'You? I'd just heard you say you were in love with my husband, what kind of a conversation was I supposed to have with you? And I'd already been that route with Geena and that didn't get me anywhere. No, it was easier to tell Archie. He already had most of the picture, I was just colouring it in for him and anyway it meant I could hurt you too this way, at least allow me that.'

'How did he take it?'

'How d'you think he took it, he was knocked out poor guy. He wouldn't believe me at first but then it all seemed to add up for him, he's not stupid. Aren't you even a little bit curious about how I came to know about you and Jack?'

'He told you?'

'No Ali, you told me. I overheard your conversation with Lauren the morning after the power outage. You know lady if you're going to sit on your balcony and talk about the guy downstairs you should at least make sure his wife's not reading her book on the sun bed first. Christ I felt betrayed and a darn fool for pouring my heart out to you. How stupid am I? First I find out about Geena, then a couple weeks later I find out about you.'

'I'm sorry.' She knew it could never be enough. 'I really am so sorry it happened.'

'That what happened? The New York affair or the one you had here last week?'

'Both of them actually.' She couldn't believe she'd said that, it sounded almost flippant. 'It's a real mess. I wish I could change things but I can't.'

'Don't beat yourself up over it.' It was a strange thing to say, she got up to leave.

'You should tell John you know about Geena and about me.'

'He's Jack by the way and why should I bother, I expect you've already filled him in?'

'Only just.'

' "Only just?" What took you so long?'

'He deceived me too you know.'

'I guess so but you can ditch the sisterhood act.'

'You're a strange one Milva, one minute you're playing the loud-mouthed American and the next it's almost like you refuse to face up to what's happened here. I mean what was it you said to Lauren when she agonised over the history of the island? "ask him the question kid" you said "it's the only way you'll get any answers." Don't you think it's time?'

'And did she take my advice?'

'Actually no, I don't think she did.'

'And what's changed?'

'Well nothing really.'

'And that's my point, some things are better left buried. I love Jack and I don't want to spend the rest of my life without him. I guess he's my *rail table* Ali and I intend to hang on to him.'

EIGHTEEN

'Christ mum that all sounds sickeningly cordial. I'd have thought she might have at least decked you or something. It must have felt weird having a civilised conversation with her about your lover, her husband.' They were in the room waiting for their bags to be collected. Robert and Archie were just leaving for the airport but going via Archie's house and Robert was promising to visit frequently during his time in the States. 'It's funny isn't it everyone seems to have ended up liking Archie, apart from you that is.'

'What do you mean? I do like Archie, I'm just not sure whether I love him that's all.' They both walked out onto the balcony to take one last look at the view. 'The truth of it is he helped me get back on my feet after dad left.'

'So you were just feeling grateful' Lauren linked arms with her mother. Alison felt this was as close as they had ever been.

'No that's a bit harsh. Not just grateful. He definitely meant something to me. Well, means something to me still but not the kind of something that makes me want to spend the rest of my life with him.'

'And what you're saying is you might not have realised that if you and John hadn't met up again?'

'Probably. It was the way I felt when I saw John again. I recognised those old feelings, that passion and saw it was missing in my relationship with Archie. Do you think that makes me an awful person?'

'I don't think you're awful mum. Bit fucked up maybe.'

'Thanks Lauren. That's a great help.' Lauren giggled.

'Will you let Archie know what Milva told you last night?'

'There's no point, I doubt he'd want to go over it again and I certainly don't.'

'Suppose. He pays for you and your daughter to come on holiday to this lovely island and you reward him by shagging the bloke downstairs. Yeah, I can see why you wouldn't want to bring it up.'

'You're really making me feel better daughter dear.'

'We've been through this before mum, that's not my job.' She squeezed her mother's arm. 'So what will you do now, now that there's no you and Archie or you and Jack to focus on?'

'What do you mean I've still got you.'

'You're not going all needy on me are you mum?' There was a knock on the door and the porter came in to collect their cases.

When she got to the bottom of the stairs Alison saw that Jack and Milva's room had been vacated. The door was wide open and she wandered in.

'They must have left really early mum, I didn't hear them leave.'

The drapes were still closed and all the drawers were pulled out as though they had left in a hurry. Alison tried to guess what might have happened but saw the bed had been slept in, on both sides.

'Hey you don't think she's drowned him in the bath' said Lauren peering into the bathroom. 'No, worse luck. Looks like he's done a runner again, mum.'

Alison looked around. 'I preferred our room.' Then taking Lauren's arm she pulled her daughter outside. 'Time to go home I think sweetheart.'

THE END

Printed in Dunstable, United Kingdom

63458291R00080